Managers and Missionaries:

Library Services to Children and Young Adults in the Information Age

LESLIE EDMONDS

Editor

University of Illinois
Graduate School of Library and Information Science
Urbana-Champaign, Illinois

ALLERTON PARK INSTITUTE

Number 28

Papers Presented at the Allerton Park Institute

Sponsored by

University of Illinois
Graduate School of Library and Information Science

Cosponsored by

The Youth Divisions of the American Library Association:
American Association of School Librarians (AASL)
Association for Library Service to Children (ALSC)
Young Adult Services Division (YASD)

held

November 14-16, 1986
Chancellor Hotel & Conference Center
1501 S. Neil
Champaign, Illinois

ISBN 0-87845-075-0   ISSN 0536-4604

CONTENTS

Introduction

The 1986 Allerton Institute was developed to provide a forum for discussion of theories and means of meeting the information needs of children and young adults in both school and public library settings. The institute was cosponsored by the Graduate School of Library and Information Science, University of Illinois at Urbana-Champaign and the three youth divisions of the American Library Association (ALA): the American Association of School Librarians (AASL), the Association for Library Service to Children (ALSC), and the Young Adult Services Division (YASD). The conference was supported by the World Book—ALA Goal Award and twenty Illinois participants received grants from the Illinois State Library to enable their attendance at the conference. The conference program was developed with the particular help of Ann Weeks and Evelyn Shaevel, both of ALA.

Speakers gave an overview of issues in the field of youth librarianship and presented perspectives on specific issues challenging librarians and media specialists. Speakers and conference participants worked together to determine directions and strategies for the profession as we look to a changing information environment in the years to come.

Four focus areas were the basis of the presentations. The papers that follow were written and presented by nationally-known leaders and are meant to provide a summary of activity in the field. The four focus areas are: (1) management of youth services, (2) recruitment and education for children's and young adult specialists, (3) evaluation of services to children and young adults, and (4) the development of a "Youth Agenda" for the youth divisions of the American Library Association and the profession.

The idea of a national conference grew out of a concern that we have a paucity of comprehensive and serious treatment of issues in the field of

1

youth librarianship. The previous 1977 Allerton Institute addressed the status of children's services in public library settings. All three youth divisions of ALA regularly address the issues of importance to each of their constituencies. There seemed to be few opportunities to address issues across age and type of library boundaries. This Allerton Institute was created to give both practitioners and academics a forum to address professional topics and to delineate areas of concern, problems in the field, and direction for professional activity as we approach a new century and a new and changing information environment.

Marilyn Miller, in her keynote presentation, gives an insightful overview of the issues likely to be facing us in providing library service to youth in the twenty-first century. She draws both on her background as a leader both in AASL and ALSC as well as thoughtful consideration of current library practice to present an analysis of information services to young people in the next twenty years.

Regina Minudri, director of the Berkeley Public Library and president of the American Library Association, draws on her experience as a youth librarian and manager of a major public library to set out issues in management of youth services. Julie Cummins presents issues in the design of services to youth; Christy Tyson addresses issues of image, cooperation, and coalition building for youth service; and Frances McDonald explores access to information and youth rights. Susan Rosenzweig and Ruth Faklis address needs for funding for services to youth, and Craighton Hippenhammer presents a model for marketing youth services effectively.

The second area of focus is presented by Margaret Bush. She deals with issues of preparation and career development of professionals who serve youth. Special issues in library education are presented by: Joan Atkinson, who discusses standards and performance appraisal of personnel; Jana Varlejs, who presents issues in the need for and delivery of continuing education; and by Margaret Kimmel, who provides demographic information on the profession. Also presented is an analysis of library education by Helen Snoke, from the School of Library Science at the University of Michigan; Judith Drescher, director of Memphis-Shelby County Public Library; and Delores Pretlow, Media Center coordinator for the Richmond, Virginia Public Schools.

In the important area of evaluation of service to children and young adults, Gerald Hodges presents various measures of service as well as issues in the field of measurement. Dawn Heller articulates areas of concern expressed by conference participants which have been the basis of goal development for the ALA youth divisions.

The ALA youth divisions responded to the recommendations from this Allerton Institute by creating the Allerton/Alliance Joint Youth Divisions Task Force. The task force had representatives from each youth division, and each member had attended the 1986 Allerton Institute. The task force was charged with the creation of a position paper based on the Allerton Institute and the *Alliance for Excellence Task Force Report.* The report of the Allerton/Alliance Joint Youth Divisions Task Force was submitted to the Joint Youth Divisions Executive Committee at the ALA Annual Conference in New Orleans in July 1988. The recommendations of this task force were for the adoption of the task force report by the youth divisions of the ALA and ALA Council and that an ALA task force be appointed to draft an implementation plan for the recommendations of the task force.

The premise of this Allerton Institute and for the subsequent work of the Task Force is that the quality of service provided by libraries and media centers is important to the social, cultural, and intellectual life of the youth served. Further, it is the responsibility of librarians serving youth to be advocates for excellent service to young patrons. It is the role of the American Library Association to provide leadership and education to youth services librarians so that they are prepared to be effective service providers in the complex, technological information environment of the society of the future.

It is through the interweaving of these elements and responsibilities that progress in youth services will be made. It is hoped that this Allerton Institute and the published proceedings will be important steps in addressing the issues facing the field on a national level. We need to look carefully at ourselves, our institutions, and youth themselves from the varying perspectives of supervisors, grassroots service providers, the professional association, and library educators. This institute was the work of many people, planners, speakers, and participants and as such represents a coalition of individuals who can contribute to the growth and change of library service to youth as we move toward the twenty-first century.

LESLIE EDMONDS
Editor

MARILYN L. MILLER

Professor and Chair
Department of Information and Library Studies
University of North Carolina
Greensboro, North Carolina

Changing Priorities for Service to Children and Adolescents in School and Public Libraries

This paper is an attempt to present some issues and concerns that will have to be addressed as continued plans are made for library programs for young people that will serve them effectively in the coming decade.

This Allerton Institute is a milestone in the history of the development of library service to American youth. What is now organized as three youth divisions of the American Library Association (ALA)—The American Association of School Librarians (AASL), The Association for Library Service to Children (ALSC), and The Young Adult Services Division (YASD)—was at one time a single body representing all youth services. Youth services librarians worked together originally as an organized, integrated group. They separated thirty-five years ago to develop unique areas of specialization by type of library and age level. Now in a different and fast changing period of time, youth services librarians are being forced to confront the inescapable fact that they may have to come together again in some way to provide more effective service to a shrinking youth population beset by tremendous social and cultural change and unrelenting rapid technological development.

Organizationally, youth services librarians have tried for the past several years to have more jointly sponsored programs at national conferences. ALA candidates and forums have been sponsored at the ALA Midwinter meetings, the three executive committees have met regularly twice a year to discuss ways of cooperating and positions that might be taken for a political impact on ALA. Overlapping services and activities are beginning to be thought of as possibilities for cooperation—ideas coming from the Alliance for Excellence and joint publications. And on the home front in various cities and small towns across the country, there have been

5

cooperative efforts at book evaluation and selection, union catalogs, resource sharing, homework hotlines, school visits, and public library field trips. All of these things have been and are good, and these must neither be denigrated nor stopped. However, it is suggested that the time has come to confront strategies and methods, prejudices, and territorial imperatives and to look at some changing priorities for delivering library service to the young. From that effort, youth services librarians could develop heightened understandings of each other and those served, decide to pool efforts, to share expertise, and to plan more effectively to improve both organizational efforts and program delivery in more home communities than is now done.

Library services are offered within a social context. The society that is shaping the current crop of children is very different from the society most of us grew up in. Children now sitting in preschools will graduate in the year 2001. They will not remember a time without computers and VCRs. The children we are talking about serving in the next fifteen years will be confronted by unrelenting and rapid changes in the demographic composition of society, family structure, schooling, and technology. In addition, the changing economy, with its developing global nature, especially a transnational work force competition that is forcing a national move away from an emphasis on an indigenous skilled blue collar work force and small family farms, forms a backdrop against which all other social issues swirl and take shape.

Demographics must be considered in designing future library service to youth. Census statistics reveal that, in general, we will have an older population, fewer children, and a different ethnic mix. The traditional nuclear family has broken up, and many single parent homes managed by women are homes of poverty. Specifically, the ethnic/linguistic composition of the population is changing rapidly and drastically. The birthrate for white women in the United States has dropped from a peak of 2.9 children per woman during the baby boom era to 1.7 in 1984. In comparison to 1970, there are some 100,000 fewer white children under the age of five and 280,000 more black children. The fastest growing minority group is Mexican-American, whose birthrate of 2.9 children per woman is currently the highest in the nation. (Asian-American populations are also growing rapidly but because of immigration and not birthrates.) In 1985, two-thirds of all immigration in the world was to the United States. The first institution to receive the children of these immigrants is the school, the second is the church, and it is hoped that the third is the public library. Fully 27 percent of all public school students in the United States represent minorities, and each of the nation's twenty-four largest city school systems has a "minority majority." By approximately the year 2010, one of every three Americans will be black, Hispanic, or Asian-American.

In 1983, for the first time in history, there were more people over 65 than there were teenagers. Of the 24 million Americans over 65, 2.2 million are over 85 and 30,000 are over 100. One forecaster has predicted that by the year 2000 there will be over 100,000 people over 100 years of age. In essence we are talking about a smaller generation of workers containing a larger percentage of women and minorities that must supply the financial support for not only a huge number of retired parents and grandparents but for the public schools and libraries and other public institutions that serve the young. Every forecaster reminds us that youth will become relatively scarce. Children will truly become national treasures eagerly recruited by colleges, the military, and employers. (McDonald's, I was told last spring on a professional visit to Connecticut, now buses teenagers from the Bronx into Connecticut suburbs to keep the glow on the golden arches and the eggs in the McMuffins.) Tomorrow's children will have even more opportunities (or problems) than their predecessors.

A few years ago, this author saw a fascinating film for the teaching of visual literacy. One section of the film had pulled together a montage of television commercials depicting the typical American family as portrayed by cereal and Jello commercials in the fifties. The typical Jello family— father in business suit, mother in pretty dress with two children (a boy child and a girl child) all sitting at a formally laid dining room table having, of course, good conversation about the day's activities as they consumed a well-balanced meal of salad, meat, vegetable, potato, and dessert (Jello, of course). That two-child, two-parent family doesn't exist anymore. Urie Bronfenbrenner (1977) stated unequivocably in a report ten years ago that: "The family is not currently a social unit we value or support" (p. 39).

Although the present administration would have us believe otherwise, the devastating cuts in human aid programs give lie to the word. And the shunning by adolescents of adult family contact, advice, and company for the sharing of ignorance and myth of their peers is a concern addressed by few. The partial results of this contemporary youth society and the breakdown of the family unit and support systems can be seen in the 9,000 teenage suicides, the majority of whom, some say, are gifted and talented, and the 25,000 deaths by automobile in 1985 alone—a total of 34,000 teenagers. This is more teenagers than attend the high schools in the Durham, Raleigh, Chapel Hill area.

Of today's children, 14 percent are illegitimate, 40 percent will be living with a single parent by their eighteenth birthday, 30 percent are latchkey children, and 20 percent live in poverty. One-third of all American children will experience poverty sometime before reaching adulthood. Fifteen percent of today's children speak another language, 15 percent have physical or mental handicaps (Hodgkinson, 1986), and 10 percent have poorly educated parents. Fifty percent of children under six have working mothers while 60 percent of children ages 6-17 have working mothers (U.S. Bureau of the Census, 1985, p. 6).

As we all know full well, the educational pendulum swings back and forth with great regularity in this country. The blessing and the curse of living in a democracy. The populace, it must be admitted, is fickle when it comes to dealing with social issues. Attention is short-lived and easily deflected. That is, of course, why missionaries are needed to keep the faith and remain steady to the resolve even when the public's attention is diverted. When the pendulum sweep starts back, the missionaries are ready to lead the forward motion.

The problems facing education are disquieting. This is really not new considering the function of schools. But concern today is about the inequities brought about by a philosophy that views an interstate highway system as federally fundable but not a fiscal floor for educational budgets to ensure a national minimum access to educational equity. Experts seem to agree that in addition to diminishing financial resources, there will be declining enrollment along with substantial shifts in enrollment at all levels of education. Some say the dropout problem will disappear in the next fifteen years because the job market and the military will be so hungry for the young that those disaffected with formal education will simply disappear and continue their learning in the informal educational institutions unbothered by the formal educational power structure because they are "off the streets."

There is no doubt that a power struggle for control of the curriculum exists. Who will determine what texts are to be used? What subject matter is to be taught? Schools have traditionally taught the values of the culture, thus they are always a little behind, and when values shift drastically, as certain elements of society today would have us believe is happening, the schools truly get caught in the crossfire. The battle lines are being drawn all over the country on the teaching of religion, sex education, values education, and global relationships, to name only a few. During this author's tenure in education, there has been a power shift from the local community, to the state, to the federal government, back to the local community, and now seeming to shift again to local competing community groups and competing professional organizations. If the school library media specialist cannot or will not buy materials objected to by community groups, will the public library stand strong?

School faculties are graying. It is predicted that two-thirds of the current crop of school library media specialists will be gone within the decade. A few years ago the average age of teachers in San Francisco was fifty-five.

An increasingly litigious society and strident parents and students will continue to cast shadows on the desirability of remaining in the teaching profession. However, there is an exciting other side. The demand for teachers will be accompanied by a call for increasing the rigor as well as the quality of the curriculum and for teaching students to think—i.e., to select, to compare, to evaluate, to synthesize. The Association for Supervision and Curriculum Development (ASCD) is but one professional group calling for the teaching of thinking skills. ASCD is involved in a Collaborative on Teaching Thinking which is working to: (1) define thinking skills and processes, (2) encourage publishers to develop instructional materials and tests that promote student thinking, (3) establish a research agenda, (4) establish and encourage adoption of standards on teaching for preservice and inservice education of both teachers and administrators, and (5) promote teaching thinking in a national public awareness campaign (Hughes, 1986, p. 33). Librarians—both school and public—need to watch this movement in terms of both selection and programs. Materials and activities which require students to develop higher order thinking skills will be essential, and teachers will be turning to us in both schools and public libraries for those resources.

A few of the global problems that demand a well-educated and informed citizenry are a shrinking world with a burgeoning population, shortages of natural resources and a decline in food sources such as fish and fertile areas for farming, the rising tide of masses of refugees, 17 million economic and political exiles now live in a land other than their birth and thereby draw on the resources of wealthier nations.

Last, but not least, of the trends affecting the future is the rapid development of communications technology—i.e., the global village, microchip technology, publishing on demand, the digital transformation of the way messages are sent and received, new languages, read only memory discs, compact discs, handheld computers, voice activated calculators, books printed on wafers to be used in calculators (which some predict may make the necessity for learning to read and write unnecessary).

With all of these wonders, one might hasten to add that the citizenry can also be instantaneously galvanized and trivialized with the same media. The destruction of tradition, the creation of true masses, the "dumbing down" of textbooks have all become reality in the mid-1980s. Everything everybody ever knew can be stored. Data can be collected about people and their lives and hoarded away to be used in ways few dreamed could ever be possible. The poorest scholar can tap information at its creation. So impressed by microchips, information is beginning to be equated with education and knowledge. One should be reminded that technology is used to provide information that people can use to become educated and to gain knowledge so that they may live full, useful, and productive lives.

The electronic classroom of the future is here. The May-June 1986 issue of *The Futurist* (Larick, 1986, pp. 21-22) describes the first phase of the Placentia Unified School District's (Orange Co., California) development of electronic classrooms. There is a similiar installation in Michigan (described in the *School Library Journal* by the library media director, Bernice Lamkin [1986]) an installation that is being replicated in a large number of high school renovations all over the country. These systems coordinate multiple technologies—i.e., satellite-delivered instructional programming, laser discs, computers, videocassettes, and closed-circuit television. The coordinated system can be directed and monitored from a central workstation. Information can be obtained from international, national, regional, and local databases via microwave, cable, telephone, or fiber optics and put into the district resource computer from which it can be transmitted to classrooms upon request (Larick, 1986, p. 22).

Against this backdrop of reality is changing demographics, shrinking financial resources, continued debate on education and its problems and strategies, and continued revolution in communications technology. How should goals and priorities be examined? The next step is to examine what is to be done based on demonstrated need and then decide how to do it. First it is decided what can be done to help this nation become a nation of readers. Then the approaches are examined: collections, coalitions, community education to support the effort, and strategies to get children to recognize the importance of reading and to want to read. Then available resources needed to accomplish the task are examined—e.g., personnel, other community agencies, collections, funding. Then strategies are developed for meeting the shortfall—i.e., acquisition of different kinds of materials, staff development, development of a volunteer cadre, community publicity, and legislative lobbying. The overriding concern is to answer the question: "How can we best effect the delivery of information and educational programs to the young that will enhance their growth and development into healthy productive citizens of a democratic society?" The following goals should be considered as deliberations are begun on new priorities:

—Attack the aliteracy problem. Work with those who know how to read but do not (an adolescent problem that one Westchester County library manager who is an active spokesperson for service to young adults told me recently is the most critical information/education problem facing educators who work with teenagers).

—Participate in the teaching of basic information skills.

—Assist in the teaching of critical thinking skills.

—Help immigrants maintain their culture.

—Advocate services by other agencies and support those services with information resources.

—Raise literacy. Support adult literacy programs.

—Support/implement, enrich, and extend school curricula.

—Shelter/after-school activities—i.e., provide a safe place.

—Provide materials for counseling—i.e., bibliotherapeutic use.

—Make common knowledge of society available in appropriate forms.

—Provide services to unserved groups in the population.

—Provide referral services to other human services agencies.

—Provide information on social and medical problems of concern to the young.

—Be more effective in working with adults who work with children—i.e., parents, teachers, grandparents, social workers.

As these priorities are discussed and fleshed out, arguments to consider are: (1) missions: where, as type of library, youth services librarians differ and where they support each other; (2) patterns of service and collection development; (3) recruitment and library education efforts; and (4) the possibilities of forming coalitions.

As these missions are considered, remember that both school and public libraries are educational institutions. The school library is concerned with both the schooling of the young and their education. The public library which has traditionally seen itself as an educational institution has also felt that it offered these experiences informally and voluntarily. The serendipity of the public library experience is truly one of the most intriguing aspects of the library for those who use it well. But if a coalition to improve information services is going to be formed, public librarians need to cast off the idea that curriculum is a word or process that is to be avoided. For some the definition of *curriculum* as planned learning experiences suffices to begin a discussion. Both school and public librarians serving youth must be cognizant of what is being planned and taught in the schools if collections are to be developed that serve the information, learning, and developmental needs of children.

One major thing that prevents moving comfortably into this arena of joint understanding is a tension between school and public library service to children that is untenable as youth services librarians plan for the future. This tension needs to be resolved by a recognition of that tension—i.e., its roots and its counterproductivity.

Braverman (1979) traces this tension back at least to 1913—the year that Edwin White Gaillard was eased out of his New York Public Library job as superintendent of work with the public schools and Anne Carroll Moore brought all services to children under her jurisdiction. As Braverman notes, the roots of this tension are both economic and philosophic, and since the real disagreements and uneasinesses are tacit and often unrecognized, it is possible for most to pay lip service to the ideal of cooperation between school and public libraries, but it may not be possible to cooperate without first confronting a few personal implicit beliefs. As Braverman (1979) documents this period, she notes that Gaillard "worked systematically to bring library resources to the schools, which then had few library services. [This] included supplying classroom collections and help to teachers, the setting up of a model school library, as well as providing reference services for students, special collections for teachers and class visits to the branches" (p. 16). Apparently, reports Braverman, Gaillard's jurisdiction overlapped with Moore's more than his philosophy did. "Moore thought that libraries should be used informally and voluntarily to promote the joy of reading" (p. 17). What a shame that a mission statement that encompassed all of those objectives could not be hammered out except for the interactions or lack of interactions and communication of those early leaders.

On a personal note, one of the genuinely exciting events of being president of ALSC was participating in a U.S. mission to visit children's libraries in the U.S.S.R. Participants visited many public libraries, some school libraries, and trade union and pioneer palace libraries. The first goal of all libraries in the U.S.S.R. that serve children is to support and encourage children to read and to see that the materials necessary to complete school assignments are available. Soviet librarians have organized study areas in public libraries, and public and pioneer palace libraries have reserve school and text collections. It was emphasized over and over again how important it is for children to learn to read and to want to read. It is not suggested that present models be replaced with the Soviet model, but it is suggested that programs developed in isolation from each other do not serve youth well.

In the United States, people are socialized by separate organizations, separate association journals, and separate library school classes, and by careful distinctions made by commission or omission. Through socialization, a blend of routines, ideals, selection techniques, programming habits, and expectations are acquired. Things are learned that conflict and which cannot be believed simultaneously with any logic, but youth services librarians go on believing them because they are too busy even to notice that they have been learned.

Patterns of service and collection development in school and public libraries must be reviewed in terms of resource sharing demanded by diminishing financial resources and continued acceleration of information produced by research, discovery, and publication by scholars, creative artists, industry, and groups of citizens demanding to be heard. Acquisition of materials based on an identification of information, idea, and knowledge needs determined by educational and developmental needs of users is crucial. A view of nonfiction collections that match needs shaped by sex, age, and socioeconomic condition must be developed if the young are going to find libraries truly essential. The response to a child or student who asks for a "good book" should be motivated by the need of the child and not just a personal aesthetic response to children's books. And one should pursue discussions of programs for the next century by realizing that users are immersed in a flood of information from a startlingly broad array of sources. It must be considered that without intermediaries, people can still be information poor if they do not know how to organize it for use, deal with it critically, and use it for a positive, beneficial purpose. It must also be realized that when collection development is discussed for the next century, the discussion should not be just about collections at one site. It must be known where other collections are located and how data can be acquired, repackaged, and disseminated. The consultant, facilitator, and producer roles will define youth services librarians just as much as these are the roles of the "special" librarian, for all users, regardless of age, will have options for access. This author must confess that she remains momentarily helpless—still, after all of these years—when students say they have decided to go into public library work rather than school library work because they love books so much. The future will place many different demands upon youth services librarians because of personal knowledge and abilities. "Just the books" won't be enough.

As noted earlier, curriculum is not a naughty word. Going to school is the full-time job of millions of residents in this country. These residents need good school libraries and good public libraries. They need school libraries which are available to them during the day and which are not full of organized classes teaching library skills in isolation of what is being presented in the classroom. They need public library collections that will extend and support what they are learning in school as well as provide them with the information needed to develop personally.

Public library collection development policies that on the one hand prohibit acquisitions that might support school work, but that, on the other hand, articulate the desire to serve the recreation, information, and cultural needs of children are puzzling. In reviewing several selection policies, I have found that many are vague and seemingly unresponsive to children's school needs when describing in positive terms the great informational needs of the young.

When examining policies: do they reflect the full-time work and needs of children? Do they reflect technology other than books? Are they positive supportive statements or are they too careful to list the restrictions? Are nonfiction books being recommended to an adolescent who says he/she needs a good book? Have the information needs of patrons been examined and then materials acquired? Have systems for keeping nonfiction collections up-to-date and accurate been developed? Are public and school librarians talking together in a community about sex education, child abuse, careers of the future, alternatives to a college education, drug abuse, loneliness, peer pressure, nuclear war, and terrorism? After talking about those subjects and determining what is being collected, are discussions being held about practices and patterns of program development for getting those resources used that will be mutually supportive? Are public and school librarians talking together about the fact that 34,000 teenagers died in 1985? All ills cannot be cured nor all problems solved, but the potential in contributing to answers and solutions for some should at least be rethought.

Public library service to adolescents as dreamed of in the fifties, sixties, and seventies is not to be—at least in this century. The realities of school, work, social pressures, and communications technology confront the avowed mission to adolescents with too much to overcome. Youth services librarians should face this fact. Public library directors have had to make choices, and they have dared to allocate this specialization to school librarians, and they have gotten away with it. It is hoped, however, that there will always be public librarians with a passion and a concern for serving adolescents and that they also will provide leadership through ALA in some organized form both to make certain that public libraries are serving the information resource needs of these young people. It is hoped they will care also about the library service in the secondary schools.

The question nagging at many youth services librarians is: where are the next decades' youth services librarians coming from? In my own state, the gains made in the seventies in staffing professional children's librarians in public libraries is being eroded: lower salaries than the public schools, lower salaries than surrounding states, and a desire to be part of a career ladder are taking their toll. All are familiar with the public school situation—i.e., the shunning of education by the bright, the variety of career opportunities now open to women, and the alarming retirement projections for school library media specialists. Where youth specialists will be educated is slightly less a concern than wondering about their recruitment. Accredited library schools continue to be dismantled—one closing announced this fall and one undergoing the type of program evaluation that has typically led to closure. The American Library Association has been strangely silent about this phenomenon. In the meantime, small unaccredited programs in schools of education in small colleges and universities all over the country are producing large numbers of school library media specialists entering the field. At this writing neither ALA nor any of its divisions has any input into the evaluation and guidance of the development and implementation of these programs. With the closure of programs has gone the opportunity to provide professional public library directors and children's librarians for many small public libraries, and with the draining of the pool of qualified librarians goes access. If the American Library Association is not going to promote education for the operation of tomorrow's libraries, then it should at least be proposing to study alternatives for the training of those who will be organizing information for delivery to various communities.

Certainly we are beginning to forge coalitions by coming here and thinking about the future as public and school library media specialists. It is believed, however, that the leadership of the youth professions should move more publicly and diligently to identify mutual concerns with other educational and helping professions. School library media specialists are coming to see that they can reach more young people if they work more diligently with the teachers. Public librarians may serve more children and adolescents also if they make more contacts with adult youth workers in the community. It was made clear during this Allerton Institute that the terrible struggle for First Amendment survival is going to be won only if coalitions are forged between and among organizations, professions, and the general public. The struggle to produce physically and mentally healthy young adults will take a coalition of social and public health workers, service groups, the law, educators, information specialists, librarians, and governments. Should we not begin to identify and promote some models at the national and state levels to help communities develop some of the same sorts of working and sharing relationships?

There are wonderful public and private schools in this country. There are outstanding public library and school library media programs across the nation. They set the pace and demonstrate excellence. But as we look ahead to the challenge of providing leadership to the next generation of librarians who will serve different constituencies than have many of us in a world that has undergone radical social change, there are things we must address. It is hoped that this conference will produce new mandates for library school researchers, the managers, and the missionaries. The mandate is to examine the mission, the collections, access and adequate staffing, the response to emerging technologies, and cooperative efforts.

The goal should be to have library/media/information services to the young directed by a professional. As a profession, answers must be found to the questions of staffing, educating, and recruiting able people and then work to provide structure to enable the service provider to offer youth the best in library/media services.

NOTES

Braverman, M. (1979). *Youth, society, and the public library*. Chicago: ALA.

Bronfenbrenner, U. (1977, February). Disturbing changes in the American family. *Education Digest, 42*, 22-25.

Hodgkinson, H. L. (1986, January). What's ahead for education? *Principal, 65*(3).

Hughes, C. S. (1986, Fall). Teaching strategies for developing student thinking: Strategies for teachers and for library media specialists. *School Library Media Quarterly, 15*(1), 33-36.

Lamkin, B. (1986, November). A media center for the 21st century. *School Library Media Quarterly, 33*(3), 25-29.

Larick, K. T. Jr., & Fischer, J. (1986, May/June). *The Futurist, 20*(3), 21-22.

U.S. Bureau of the Census. (1985). *Statistical abstract of the United States: 1986* (106th Ed.). Washington, DC: USGPO.

REGINA MINUDRI

President, American Library Association
Director, Berkeley (California) Public Library

Management of Youth Services:
Political, Financial, and Social Implications

Why is it so hard to convince people—adult people—that children are important and that they are the brightest and need the best? Why do we continually undervalue those who serve children, those who teach children, and those who care for children? Why must libraries, schools, and other educational institutions beg for crumbs while society force feeds the bloated military/industrial complex? Why do aging leaders forget that youths die when nations fight? Why is the future mortgaged to pay for the fantasies of the past?

Implications of the Management of Youth Services

It is interesting to note the order in which these implications are presented. Five years ago we might have seen the fiscal side head the list. Ten years ago there was a fascination with social implications and societal changes. Today politics takes first position. That observation is not meant to imply that political considerations are more important than those of the budget or those of the surrounding communities, but it is the juxtaposition that interests this author.

For decades youth services librarians have been missionaries in the most generic sense. Our foremothers worked long and hard to establish the importance of library services to young people, to establish patterns and methods of serving youth, to communicate a strong sense of commitment, and provide a solid philosophical base. For many years these dedicated individuals toiled hard in the fields nurturing, pruning, weeding, and tending the garden. They made it possible to develop means and methods for today. Youth services librarians owe them a very large debt.

The only way that debt to our foremothers can be paid is to guarantee that quality library services to children and youth continue to exist and, in fact, continue to grow and develop. We know that children are the future of

17

the world. We know that just as there is a debt to the past, there is an equal debt to the future. This debt must be repaid in the form of a legacy of superior library services, of humanistic and careful administration, and of institutions which respond easily and quickly to user needs. It is important that we work hard to pave the way for the librarians who will follow; the librarians who will continue the job after we are long gone.

Political Implications

The political implications of life in the 1980s and 1990s force us to recognize where funding responsibilities lie, how these can be understood, how these can be affected, and how best to position youth services so that adequate financial resources allow the provision of superior services. Lots of folks say that they don't want to be bothered with political activity, that it is too time-consuming, that it doesn't have anything to do with their chosen field of endeavor, etc.

Youth services librarians serve the most visible and most vocal clientele in all of libraryland. Children are the most photogenic of library users. They are cute and just about everyone agrees that children are important. The job is to get people to put their money where their mouths are and establish priorities that serve youth well. That requires political considerations.

So often it appears as though we forget what truly useful skills youth services librarians possess. It is easy to use publicity skills and promotional abilities. To begin with, see to it that flyers announcing programs are always sent to library management trustees, city councils, and other governmental agencies. Invite politicos to awards ceremonies. Be sure to have a photographer there to take pictures, and be sure that the politicos are aware that a photographer will be there. Don't forget the effectiveness of the kissing babies syndrome. Post the photographs and send them to the media. It is assumed here that you know what to send, where to send it, and who will help to get it published.

Lobbying and political strategies are mostly common sense. Remember that strength is in numbers and that real strength lies in affiliating with others who have similar interests. When E.J. Josey used coalitions as the theme for his ALA presidential year, he really had the right idea. It is important that legislators, no matter at what level—local, regional, state, or national—see that there is a community of interest and broad support for the issues we champion. There are the obvious cohorts such as child care providers, schools, recreation centers, and the not-so-obvious like senior centers, health care providers, social workers, booksellers, local chambers of commerce, and the like. You can find common ground with just about all these folks, they can support you, and you can support them. That is what coalition building is all about.

It is also important that we keep ourselves well informed, that we inform allies, and that we speak, if not always with one voice, then at least in the same key. Be logical, know the issues, and know the interests of your legislators. Don't worry if, when you call, you speak to an aide. It is often a legislator's aide that makes decisions, assists in making policy, and advises the boss.

Be more than a single issue person (you will find yourself doing this as you build coalitions). It is important that you watch and read so you are aware of where your legislator stands. It is helpful to be able to refer to some earlier action of the legislator that you liked, some issue on which you agree with her/him.

If a legislator does right by you, send thanks. Let the legislator know that you appreciate the help and that you recognize the good he or she has done. Remember that we often complain and rarely compliment elected officials. They are human too and certainly appreciate knowing that somebody likes what they are doing just as you would if you were in that position. A brief note will do.

Utilize library support groups like Friends of the Library. Everybody needs friends, and thank God that libraries have them. Friends of the Library are often listened to better than librarians because they are not perceived to have a vested interest. Local officials therefore consider them to be concerned and motivated citizens and pay attention to them. Don't ever underestimate the power of a vocal, well-informed citizenry on any elected official. Therefore be sure that your Friends of the Library are well-informed and are kept up to date. They are extremely valuable to any library. If you think all of this takes a lot of work, you're right. If you think you may not be able to do it on work time, you're right. If you think it is a long row to hoe, you're right.

Two heartening victories in California demonstrated how important all these lobbying efforts are:

1. In Berkeley after Proposition 13 we passed a local tax measure to support the public library. It was a massive effort with much work from the library staff, the Friends of the Library, and many interested local folks. We passed the measure with 68 percent of the vote. It's good for ten years and during the life of the measure it will bring in over 30 million new dollars to the library. Not bad for a first effort. We are now planning for the renewal and continuance of the library tax in 1988. We have begun the effort to involve the Berkeley community at the primary planning level and are in the process of identifying critical issues and long-range needs for the library and its services.

2. In 1983 California's legislature created the Public Library Fund, an act which gave per capita support to the state's public libraries for the first time. In 1983 it was $6 million, in 1984 $12 million, in 1985 $18 million,

and we anticipate approximately $20-22 million in 1986. All for public libraries.

Neither of these efforts could have been achieved without massive efforts on the part of those involved. They would have been impossible without the help and support of the citizenry at large who perceived that public libraries were a public good and believed that the state had and continues to have a statewide responsibility to public libraries. State support of libraries—public, academic, and school—is critical to development, growth, networking, resource sharing. Youth services must be involved in these plans and represent the needs of their clientele.

There are a couple of questions for you. How many of you know: Who your mayor is? Who the members of the City Council are? Members of County Boards? State Assemblyman? State Senator? U.S. Congressperson? U.S. Senator? It is good to know who these people are and how to reach them. Also, how many of them know you? Think about that for a moment.

We are aware of the past, know the present, and must be ready for the future. Because of special skills, knowledge, and abilities, we have a debt to the future that cannot be minimized. People do what they want to do. We achieve what we want to achieve. Our potential is truly boundless. We have the resources and the intelligence. We also have the drive and the need. All we need now is to go out and do it.

Financial Implications

Budgets are compilations of numbers. They are meant to help, to assist, and to guide. They are often used to distract, to restrain, to compel, and to obstruct. Budgets can be what you make of them. Remember that while numbers may not lie, numbers don't always tell the whole truth.

A budget is a true test of priorities. No matter what people might say about how important something is, you must always look at how they spend their money in order to get a clear picture of what is really important. Just take a look at the federal budget and see how much importance the present administration places on education, the ecology, and defense. Your library's budget will demonstrate clearly the library's priorities no matter what the stated objectives may be. As the budget is examined in this light, many will recognize that this is an uphill battle. It is here that internal coalitions and internal political activity develops between library units, divisions, and departments.

Just as we use intelligence in the external political arena, so it is necessary to know how things work internally—i.e., inside the bureaucratic institutions. The same rules apply. No matter what the library setting is like, it will have its own set of internal political considerations. It is important to develop the ability to lobby, form coalitions, understand climates, communicate effectively, and work within your own bureaucracy.

No one can afford to be isolated, or to be perceived as being isolated or aloof. Today the team or task force approach to problem solving lends itself well to increased multilevel participation in the quest for solutions. Recognize the inherent truth in the old adage that if you are not part of the solution you are part of the problem.

Gathering information, building bridges, and communicating needs are activities that help. You must know who to talk to and when, you must understand how to present your needs, how to defend them, how to justify them, and how to relate them to the overall goals and objectives of the library.

As you enter this arena you need to know how to play the game, the lingo, and the rules. You need to know the box scores, the batting averages, the handicaps, etc. Learn the rules. When I first became an administrator, I was often asked why. Why did I leave the front lines of library service and ensconce myself behind a desk protected by a secretary and inaccessible to the public? Why indeed? I became an administrator because I thought I could do the job and because I felt I had a mission, a challenge, and a goal of superior service. I hoped to make the library responsive, user-friendly, and an integral part of the community it serves. I also hoped to enable the staff to provide the highest possible level of library services.

This is not a challenge that can be met in a single summer but rather takes a lot of winters, autumns, springs, and summers. It takes time, effort, energy, persistence, tenacity, and sometimes sheer dumb stubbornness. A good manager must not be afraid to make mistakes or be controversial. As my mother once said when I complained about controversy and hassle: if you don't have controversy, maybe nothing vital is happening. You're doing nothing new, no changes are taking place. Nothing risked is nothing gained.

What do you need to know about administration in order to survive and to become more vital and viable? First, you have to know the ropes. You have to become aware of the atmosphere, the milieu, the vibes. It is important that you have the ability to speak the language when you visit foreign climes, or you'll never be understood by the natives, and for sure you'll never find the secret passageways to the treasure vaults. Budget processes generally run throughout the year and it is not unusual for administration to be working simultaneously on three or even four fiscal years. It is important that the library's budget cycle is clearly understood and that the calendar of events and deadlines are kept.

When dealing with justifications, keep in mind that statements need to be phrased in the boiler plate used inside your bureaucracy. Trends exist in budgeting just as they do in fashion. Relate cause to effect, effort and person hours to quantifiable goals and measurable results. Develop proposals which enhance, enable, and extend while demonstrating a clear understanding of relationships within the bureaucracy.

Allocation of scarce resources (our resources are always scarce) is the single most important activity of library management. Personnel resources, more commonly known as people, are the most valuable resource of any library as well as the largest single expenditure—often up to 80 percent of the budget. Extreme care must be taken so that precious time is not wasted so that people are allowed to go about their work efficiently. Wasting personnel resources is like throwing money into a dustbin. In preparing proposals, take care that the right people are doing the right things at the proper levels.

There is no special club for managers, no secret handshakes, no Egyptian robes to wear. Management is a constant exercise in coping skills. The real secrets lie in understanding *where* you are going, *how* you are going to get there, *what* needs to be done, *who* will do it, and *when* to make your move. It is always necessary to be fair, direct, and honest and to treat others as you like to be treated. Common sense, imagination, and empathy serve any manager well.

Many librarians serving youth complain that they aren't taken seriously by their administrators, managers, or supervisors. It seems that we still suffer from some of the myths about youth services librarians. Following are some common myths stated in negative terms. A later discussion will show how they can be turned around and made positive. Sadly, some of these are self-perpetuating. Youth services librarians: are childlike, overly identified with client group; are incapable of seeing the big picture; don't see beyond their own services; are emotional; can't be reasoned with—are stubborn; live in an Ivory Tower; are inflexible; fluster easily; don't understand budgets; don't know how to justify requests (because they only ask for what is right, true, just, and good); can't estimate or forecast; refuse to listen to reason—won't compromise; and won't set priorities because everything is important.

Are any of these familiar? Do you recognize yourselves? It is hoped not. These myths can be turned around and viewed on the positive side and then *transferable skills* can be recognized as being possessed by those serving youth.

For example, anyone who can manage twenty hyperactive children in a story hour can work easily with a group of reasonably docile adults. Anyone who can produce flyers, bibliographies, and prepare weekly or monthly programs has already figured out how to deal with media and promotion. Anyone who can coordinate and produce summer reading programs, visits, and do booktalks to classrooms full of "spring-filled" young adults has organizational skills. Anyone who can evaluate and review thousands of books and relate them to thousands of others in the collection can certainly understand the "big picture."

It is important that we all understand and use the language of administration in order to get our points across. Fie, you may say, "don't want to learn gobbledygook like that." You had best learn this game because it's the only one in town. If you want to get what's best for your department, you really must be able to present its needs carefully, in the best possible light, to those who make the decisions.

It is equally important that you know what is going on in your own local situation. You should be aware of the political context which surrounds your library. It is important that you be cognizant of changes in income levels, education levels, population changes, things which can become predictors of future trends. We are an aging society. Population forecasts show that by the year 2000 we will have more people over sixty-five than under eighteen. These changes in population do not negate the need for quality library services to youth. You must be prepared with your justifications, your arguments, and your persuasive forces because hard questions will be asked. You will be expected to come up with the answers.

I am convinced that youth services librarians have underestimated themselves and have not recognized the transferable skills they possess. These skills make people eligible for advancement. They enable and empower, but only when the particular skills, knowledge, and abilities are recognized, are translated into the appropriate jargon, and are presented positively. It is endemic to society that those who serve children and youth are undervalued. Somehow serving children and youth is seen as less important than taking out the garbage. Anyone can do it—after all they're only kids. What a false and fruitless attitude. However, this attitude persists because we allow it. We don't sing our own praises or shout our accomplishments. If we don't care enough to take care of ourselves, how can we expect someone else to do the job for us? A skilled and talented librarian can easily have a dramatic effect on the rest of a child's life.

Women's professions are traditionally underpaid. Where is it written that a secretary should earn less than a gardener? The concept of pay equity is being heard loud and clear in our land, and women in many jurisdictions are fighting for equality, pay parity, and a larger slice of the pie. Librarians serving youth must join in this effort.

This song rings loud and clear for librarians, 80 percent of whom are women in a traditionally undervalued market. Most of us work for government. We have been patient, calm, and soft-spoken. I believe that era is over. More and more women are speaking out or are refusing to take a pat on the head and a high sounding title instead of money. We are insisting on the value of our labor and the worth of contributions to our institutions.

All librarians who occupy professional positions within a specific library should be paid on the same scale, regardless of their specialty. This seems almost too obvious to state. A librarian is a librarian no less because she happens to serve youth. In fact, children's and young adult librarians must know two collections and be able to flow easily from adult to children's materials and back again with ease; a feat not usually required of specialists in other services.

Promotion for youth services librarians generally means changing the job and leaving the specialty. I have often felt that there should be a place for advancement for persons who are expert in an area, but who do not choose to become supervisors. We are all familiar with the Peter Principle of advancement: it is almost a truism that the best person at the activity is not necessarily the best supervisor. We must begin to recognize the value of a highly skilled and trained children's or young adult librarian. These folks are worth their weight in platinum. Why can't public libraries develop a plan which could have a multitude of steps in the salary range of, say, 10 to 15 with advancement based on continuing education classes, workshops, conference attendance, and/or publication. Public schools have similar plans which allow teachers to advance through a deep salary range. I don't know of any public libraries that have attempted such a system, but it surely can be worked on from existing educational parallels.

As I look at what I consider to be promotable qualifications, I am ever drawn to the skills, knowledge, and abilities I see exhibited by competent youth services librarians. When I consider what I want to see in a branch supervisor, I look for a person who can deal with the community, who will speak out, who has a basic understanding of budget, who understands the local neighborhood and the library system, who can plan ahead, who enjoys working with people, and who is eager to forge ahead. Do you recognize any of your knowledge, skills, and abilities in what I just said? Do you try to be a part of the overall library system? Do you contribute to the myriad of committees and efforts that are taking place in your library? I believe that advancement of competent children's and young adult librarians will serve us well in the long run, putting people in charge who understand and support youth services.

I firmly believe that we must be proactive if we are to get the kind of continuing education we need and want. If what you feel is important to you is not there—seek it out. Investigate all the resources at your disposal. Talk to your colleagues and see if your system might be willing to do some in-house work and make suggestions as to the continuing education subjects in which you are interested. Monitor the activities of your local library association, your state association, and ALA. If you identify a course that you wish to take, be prepared to show how that course will help in your daily work (if you wish your library to send you and/or give you release time to attend). Also be prepared to share what you learn with your colleagues.

It is important to avoid attending the same kind of workshop or program year after year. It is tempting to attend the author luncheons, storytelling workshops, or booktalking sessions. I also know and understand how stimulating and refreshing they are and how you can return to your library re-energized, renewed, and revitalized. However, I submit that much can also be gained from things outside one's specialty. Workshops and courses on time management, budgeting, supervision, and evaluation will also give fresh insights and new approaches. You can adapt what you learn to your specific situation.

A brief word here about adaptability. Adaptation, in my opinion, is one of the great skills librarians possess. Background and training allow us to examine what others do and organize the activity to suit various situations. Concrete examples of this can be seen in the use of paperback book racks, in use of graphics, in the design of open spaces, and in the ease with which we become accurate reflectors of community's needs. I have seen librarians examine literature racks in a bank carefully and then create an adaptation for the library that works better. It is not unusual for young adult librarians to take a commercial product and fix it so it works for them. It is not only those obvious adaptative skills that are impressive, but also the constant search for better ways and improvements that has always convinced me that this profession is much more than the sum of all its parts. It is also one of the reasons that the average library is the best managed department in a city, county, or district.

I've said this before today and now I say it again. No one blows your horn accurately but you. You know all these things already. We live in an age of assertion, an age of self, and an age of proactivity. It is important that one is assertive in support of your own efforts and in support of the client group served. No one else can do it better; few others will do it at all. It is vital that management be informed of how great your service is and how wonderfully you perform your duties and meet your objectives. It is also important that youth services coordinators become part of the library's management team and take part in the decision-making process.

Social Implications

As I began to think about the social implications inherent in the management of youth services today, I thought it would be a breeze. After all, don't we always love to discuss philosophy of services, the good that these services provide, and the sheer joy with which these services are provided? I have decided that perhaps that breeze could be closer to hot air and that indeed it is time to take a new look, participate in a new vision, and bring ourselves up to speed with tomorrow.

Life in the fast lane typifies the society of the 1980s. Concorde jets decrease travel time between continents. Tape recorders can speed up speech so we can listen faster. Fast forward and rewind buttons are used constantly. Commercials break concentration patterns into twelve minute segments and batter the senses with ten second messages selling images and not products. Political leaders are packaged and sold like breakfast cereals, and no one takes time to discuss the real issues. The façade has become the reality. Individuals feel powerless and impotent. Automation controls institutions that have major impacts on life.

It is easy to focus on the difficulties of twentieth-century life and the United States in particular. It is also easy to refuse to acknowledge them. Neither path is fruitful. Neither path affords a way to make the best possible of the best available.

Librarianship is a service profession. It is a profession which enables us to use our developed skills to empower and enrich others. Librarianship is a profession which opens doors, shares knowledge, and makes information public. We are knowledge brokers in the best and most positive sense. We are not power brokers. That does not, however, make us weak. The profession has the capacity to utilize valuable information for the public good. We need to develop ways and means to ensure that the public always has access to the information and resources it needs. That is truly the dilemma this service profession faces today.

I am inordinately proud of us. I never cease marveling at our ability, our consistency, our intellectual athleticism, and our resiliency in the face of threats and cutbacks.

Librarianship is also a nurturing profession. It stands for self-development, continual learning, individual achievement, and personal curiosity. Youth services librarians continually demonstate those nurturing skills within bureaucracies. The guidance, encouragement, enthusiasm, involvement, and assistance given to youth through their libraries and their librarians bodes well for the future.

Back to the future and its social implications. As nurturers and service providers, as guides and enthusiasts, librarianship now stands at the gates of tomorrow. Whether we can make the roads clear for youth to advance easily will determine youth service librarians' value, validity, and viability.

Discussions must take place about the nature of resource sharing as it applies to children, to school libraries, and to children's materials. It is not at all uncommon to see that children and juvenile materials are excluded from interlibrary loan processes. When the formation of multitype library networks are discussed, school libraries are usually the last to be included. Generally schools are last-in because of costs, decentralization, lack of staff, and an often perceived lack of interest in the resources they can share.

The changes that affect society affect youth. How do we manage information services for youth in the waning days of the twentieth century?

How do we assure that young people have access to the information needed in this era of electronic transfer and storage of information on electronic databases? Do young people even need them? It is critical that the information needs of clients are understood. We need to be aware of how young people obtain and use information. As more information changes from print to electronic storage, we must address the needs of students at all levels and the costs of accessing the information that they need to acquire. Fees for service can make it impossible for children and young people to get desired data.

Children and young adults are creatures of their times. It is impossible to deny the impact of television on these individuals. It is also important that we recognize that a generation raised on television and computers reacts differently than one brought up without the furniture that stares back and without the appliance that interacts electronically.

I do not advocate tossing out tried and true traditional patterns of services or approaches to children's literature and interest in quality and the importance of the oral tradition of storytelling. I also believe that the level and type of library service we give to children and young people is not merely important to us; it is critical to their development and to the nation's future.

I lay before you a challenge. Assist the American Library Association to recognize and develop an agenda for the twenty-first century. This agenda will help the profession of young adult librarians to develop new service patterns for today's youth which will serve tomorrow's adult. I call upon the leadership of ALA's Youth Divisions—ALSC, AASL, and YASD—to begin a triple barreled approach to determine a road map which will help chart the course and begin to prepare for the third millenium.

Let us examine the status of youth services today, plan what it should be for tomorrow, recognize what changes have to be made, look at new service patterns, develop mission statements and goals, see how these affect library services at all levels, and provide the ALA with a position and a philosophy. I see this beginning with youth and then becoming broad based and truly representative of library services at all levels. This study must begin with youth services since these are the first to handle the diversity and complexity of the changing society through our children.

Let us walk down these new avenues together and begin to answer the questions that are only now being formulated. I know that it must be done, and I know that together we can do it.

JULIE CUMMINS

Children's Services Consultant
Monroe County Library System
Rochester, New York

Design of Youth Services

How will the public library or school media center's program of service relate to the changing needs of youth? Take the word *design*—how do you interpret it? As the grand scheme of things, the master plan, a schematic, a blueprint? A blueprint is a detailed specific set of guidelines for creating a building from paper to brick. For the purpose of this discussion, the concept of a blueprint will be used as an approach to designing youth services for a specific situation.

When a blueprint concept was selected for this presentation, actual blueprints were examined to ascertain the areas and specific components for a building. They include: elevations, roof plans, foundations, plumbing, mechanics, electrical, or source of energy. Use this approach to energize your thinking of designing service with six designated areas. Instead of citing areas identified as the living room, kitchen, bedroom, etc. for a household building, six areas are identified with specific functions which, when aligned in place with each other, comprise a total children's and young adult library service facility. They are:

> Communication Center—In Touch
> Reflections—Room of Mirrors—Image
> Information Retrieval Center—Access
> Library-Den-Study—Literacy, education
> Energy Center—Pulse, power, programs
> Community Hub—Outreach, community involvement

Communication Center

A center of communication means being in touch with your counterpart school or public librarian, parents, teachers, library administrators, trustees, and community agencies. How many times a year do you meet with your school or public librarian, have lunch together, send memos to each other, forward project plans, trade reading lists, share books and equipment, or present programs jointly?

Figure 1. Design for Youth Service

Do you offer parents evening and weekend programs on how to parent, sessions on child abduction, programs on new books for all ages, computer courses where parent and child are enrolled together, programs on how to pick a nursery school or summer camp? Youth services librarians must also be in touch with teachers. This involves honoring requests for assignments and reading lists and providing specially-planned programs on a topic such as science fairs.

Youth services librarians must also be in touch with the administration of the library. To make the administration an advocate and supporter of youth services, they must be informed of what is taking place, how services are being provided, and what is needed to meet the community's needs. Constant reminders should be made to administrators of how the children's department makes them and the library look good. Submit monthly reports, send selected new books once a month for administrators to see, provide anecdotes for the board, and report to the board on a special program with a minimum appearance of once a year.

Another group to keep in touch with is trustees. Have you taken them on a tour of the children's area or sent them copies of any booklists you've prepared? Do you know their names so you can greet them personally? Are you demonstrating in a positive, professional way that the library is not just a babysitting service for children? If the library's program of service is not up to standard, the best chance of raising it is to court the trustees.

Other agencies serving parents and youth are also important in keeping in touch with. You need to know what they are doing, and they need to be aware of the library. Have you applied jointly for grant funds to underwrite a project? Have you discussed a joint strategy for sponsoring a program?

Yes, all this sounds like you are doing it all. Even though communication is defined as being two-way, your communication signals have to be stronger and more frequent to guarantee a return of even 25 percent.

Communication is your form of commercial. It's more than public relations. It's a way of telling what you have to offer and selling your service. Think of your communication center as the hub with the spokes sending out signals to the school librarian, teachers, parents, children, administration, and agencies.

The reverse holds true for school media specialists. Are you in touch with your counterpart? Are you in touch with the parents of your students? What service are you providing for them? Are you in touch with teachers? Do they know what you can do for them? Are you in touch with your administration? Aside from all the reports you're required to submit, have you sent the administration one memo citing an especially rewarding project that took place in the media center or sent a photo of a child shown achieving a particular level of success with a computer program or learning kit for the school bulletin board?

Another group to communicate with are school board members. Do you know who they are? At an open house, have you targeted a packet of materials for them or a bookmark with their names done in computer graphics?

Service to children is the cornerstone of public library service and school education. We are creating the library users of tomorrow, the voting adults who pull the lever for library funding and school bond issues, and the future contributors to the community, state, and beyond. Communication is your form of commercial. Use it to sell your product—i.e., library service.

Reflections—Room of Mirrors

What kind of image do we convey within the profession, to other professions, and to ourselves? Numerous publications have pressed the point that it is not sufficient for children's and young adult specialists to just have skills for working with young people. They must also have training in managerial skills and must be seen and perceived as managers. Every children's specialist serves as a manager on two separate levels. One level covers the responsibilities of providing, maintaining, and utilizing a collection of materials either in the school or public library. These are the day-to-day activities involved in managing a children's library department (Cummins, 1980, pp. 7-10).

The second level of management is the children's specialist as a supervisor and a member of the management team. It is at this level, regardless of the size of the staff or library, that the children's librarian has a function and responsibility as part of the overall decision-making process that governs the library and its service. This means that you must be able to present your program of service in terms of goals and objectives and learn to use statistics to make a case; you must be able to present a budget in terms the director can use, in terms that governmental forces want to hear, and in terms that express your needs and programs convincingly. You need to be able to make a public presentation, address various kinds of boards, and talk in terms that a particular group will understand and nod in agreement.

You need to be politically savvy. The board or council as a whole determines your budget but individual members make up that board. Who knows if the father of one of your preschool children might be vice-mayor and that subtle reinforcement of the positive aspects of library programs could eventually translate into funds. The same is true for the school media specialist. Know the members of the Board of Education. The election or appointment of a librarian or Friend of the Library could provide beneficial support.

To keep your image polished requires feeling and looking alert and energized. Everyone needs stimulation to keep abreast, to be perceptive, and to be invigorated, and that requires continuing education. Reading journals and talking to peers and other librarians will provide new ideas but not to the extent and stimulation that workshops, conferences, institutes, and in-service training will.

Continuing to learn after two or twenty-two years on the job is a measure of professional attitude and commitment to the profession. Involvement in library associations is important. Just paying dues is not sufficient in terms of presenting image. Involvement builds pride in being a librarian and a youth specialist.

Information Retrieval Center

Information retrieval requires access. A multitude of information is stored in the center—how and when may young people retrieve it, and how do you as the librarian interface with it?

The first way to provide access to information is by eliminating unseen barriers. Are children able to use and borrow materials from any section of the library? Does their library card restrict them by age or grade to numbers or kinds of items they may use or borrow? Are children included in interlibrary loan (ILL) programs? Are there any rules—local or state—that eliminate them from being able to request materials on ILL? If so, they are being denied service.

The second way to retrieve information is by format. Can children use the computer in the library, can they request database searches, are they allowed the use of the microfilm reader-printer? When automation decisions are made on the administrative level, the youth specialist must insist on equal treatment and equal consideration for young people.

A third aspect of access is physical. For young children, can they reach the top shelves, especially if the juvenile nonfiction is intershelved with adult materials? Are steps, counters, and furniture scaled appropriately for primary age children? If not, when renovations, remodeling, or new buildings are planned, it is incumbent upon the children's librarian and school media specialist to provide input to those people making those types of decisions to "design" with children in mind, including placement of the children's area. Access is an important consideration. Children must have it, otherwise they are inhibited in their growth, their learning, and their attitude toward libraries.

With spoken and visual formats of information expanding broadly, another element of access comes into play. Adele Fasick, in "Moving into the Future without Losing the Past," talks about children's need to hear language and speak language as a precursor to understanding and assimilating printed language and words. Background and experience determine differing responses by children to film or print and to ways in which information is learned and received. Librarians need to be able to assess and evaluate which format is best for a specific child (Fasick 1984, pp. 405-13).

Then there is access to information for the youth services librarian. Another communication link could be formed between the school librarian and the public librarian by ordering materials via computer. If the public or school librarian can punch up a screen to see if a particular title has been ordered, that is access to information that translates into wise collection management.

If this is not feasible, does the public librarian send reports or records of selection lists or new books and nonprint acquired to the school person? Does the school media specialist in turn send lists of new software, equipment, and project assignments to the public library person?

You as the librarian are the advocate for access to information for children. Also remember that access to information for you is another interface with the whole information center.

Library—Den—Study

Literacy and education as a broad topic encompasses print literacy, visual literacy, computer literacy, and technology literacy. To keep up with children, librarians must be computer literate. Children are as comfortable using computers in various facets of their educational life as well as their home life as we were with typewriters. There is a natural affinity between students and microcomputers. The public library and the school library should serve as links between the natural desire of the child to learn about his world and the equipment necessary to accomplish it (Lintner, 1985, pp. 91-93). We need to know how to operate a computer or word processor and know what computers can do for us.

But that alone is not sufficient. The rate at which technology is changing and advancing is extremely fast. It is not conceivable that an individual children's librarian can keep pace with or on top of the newest format, the latest development, or the 8000th model of a piece of equipment, but it is conceivable—and necessary—that the youth librarian be aware of what is developing, knowing that change is constant, and being alert to updates of technology through journals and conferences.

Of course, we as librarians support literacy, but you must decide what is the library's role in helping with the literacy problem. Is it as simple as providing space for tutors to work with students, or should you be involved more directly? Philosophies differ on this issue so the critical thing is to determine the extent of the library's or system's responsibility. Provision of materials for both children and adults is basic and so is a congenial atmosphere. Is staff time also made available for them to work with tutors or student groups?

Actually, most of the programs children's librarians plan have literacy at the core—e.g., by fostering a love of books and stories, relating books with activities, exploring films and books together, sponsoring reading clubs, and so on.

Other programs that can be used to visibly promote reading in the community are read-a-thons with local celebrities, media coverage for the March of Dimes Reading Champions, and other agency campaigns. Learn to use any connections as features of literacy—e.g., local people on award committees, a local sports figure to hand out prizes or certificates at library activities, pictures of the mayor reading with his/her grandchildren or holding a favorite children's book. Use all of the available national promotions and add a local twist.

At the recent AASL conference in Minneapolis, William Bennett, the U.S. Secretary of Education, called librarians the ambassadors of literacy. He cited the most important responsibility of elementary schools is to teach children how to read and become active and avid readers (Flagg, 1986, pp. 737-739).

Dr. Seuss put it more succinctly in the new book, *Once Upon a Time,* published for the 20th anniversary of Reading is Fundamental: "The more you read, / the more things you know. / The more that you learn, / the more places you'll go" (Dr. Seuss, 1986, p. 41). Recognize that unless there is a commitment to literacy, there may be fewer and fewer readers to serve.

Energy Center

The energy center is the power behind your service, the pulse of activity that energizes program offerings. It is the "life" of the children's library in the community. The energy must come from you, the children's librarian, and from the programs you plan.

If you have had a Saturday morning film program for years and years and the attendance has dwindled from 175 kids to 25, that should tell you something. For many reasons this program no longer has the appeal it previously did—the over-familiarity of 16 mm films as a medium, passive instead of active programming, and a program format that has become routine and dull. Drop it or change it and in its place try something that involves children. All programming does not have to be passive.

Try having children make their own films. With very simple equipment, kids can draw on film, or create animation with live characters or clay figures. Do a whole animation series. Have children make flipbooks and move on to other animation forms. A show could be presented at the end of the series and maybe a local camera shop would sponsor the event or supply the equipment.

Expand your programming with other age levels. Intergenerational programs that use senior citizens with elementary age children can bring new life to both groups. Craft workshops and reading skill groups are examples, but the possibilities are extensive. In exchange, have the kids teach computer skills to the seniors. A good example of tapping the talents of senior citizens to use with children is a program created in Iowa called "From Sheep to Shirt." Members of a local weavers guild brought looms, two craftswomen brought their spinning wheels and dye pots, and a 4-H student brought her sheep to demonstrate sheep shearing. The occasion provided a first-hand experience and understanding of the fabric process for the children who attended (Irving, 1985, pp. 82-84). The goodwill and support that is gained from this approach is immeasurable—support you can't buy but is worth money on a bond issue.

Expand your programming to other agencies and institutions. Consider jointly sponsoring a program with the art or science museum. Use special exhibits for program inspiration. A dinosaur exhibit could springboard into a program of dinosaur models/stories/riddles, or a medieval festival at the gallery would be perfect for dragon tales told in both locations. A unique project could take place by applying jointly for funding from Arts Councils, Poets-in-Residence, etc. What programs can you plan with the local Association for the Education of Young Children, YWCA, or YMCA?

Expand your thinking about programs. Look for new ideas and topics that will be featured by other organizations, ways of underwriting projects that need funds, and initiate communitywide events such as read-a-thons or cosponsorship of an author-illustrator with a bookstore or PTA.

Bring technology into your programming particularly in the schools. Use interactive video to involve an entire school building in a project on reliving history or taking a trip into space. Connecting a videodisc, videotape, filmstrip, or slide projector to a microcomputer allows the student to make interactive decisions involved with a scenario (Troutner, 1983, pp. 337-340). Think of the possibilities.

Does your school or library have cable access and capabilities? Besides routine school newscasts, instructional demonstrations, and story programs, how about having students present book reviews on the air and running them as spot announcements during the day or in the school cafeteria at noon time?

The Energy Center is where things happen. It is the pulse, the power source that gives your library vitality. Make it come alive with creative, fun, and involving activities.

Community Hub

To get community involvement you need to know your community—i.e., percentages of population by age, ethnic groups, diversity, and location. What do demographics tell you about the community? What is the birthrate in your area? What ethnic group is having the most babies?

The 1980 census reveals the average white in America is thirty-one years old, the average black twenty-five, and the average Hispanic only twenty-two, which shows a definite population momentum for minorities. It indicates that the average Hispanic female is just moving into the peak childbearing years while the average white female is moving out of them (Hodgkinson, 1985, p. 3).

This is why California now has a majority of minorities in its elementary schools, while Texas schools are 46 percent minority, and half the states have public school populations that are more than 25 percent non-white, while all of the twenty-five largest city school systems have minority majorities (Hodgkinson, 1985, p. 3).

The 1980 census indicates that 59 percent of the children born in 1983 will live with only one parent before they reach eighteen—that becomes the normal childhood experience. Of every 100 children born today, twelve will be born out of wedlock, forty will be born to parents who divorce before the child is eighteen, five will be born to parents who separate, two will be born to parents of whom one will die before the child is eighteen, and forty-one will reach age eighteen "normally" (Hodgkinson, 1985, p. 3).

You don't exist without your community. Libraries are next to Mom and apple pie, but without people—children and adults—you have no business. So service is the key. Do you have a large number of families where both parents work? Has attendance at the regular morning story hour dropped because of few children or because those children are in day-care centers? Demographics indicate that the number of children eligible for Head Start type of programs will increase in the next decade as the number of children in poverty continues to expand. That number of eligible children has increased by one-third while the funding for the programs remained the same as in 1985. How does that affect preschool services in schools and public libraries? Should an evening story hour program be offered to those parents? Should the public library plan weekly sessions with Head Start, should the Head Start groups meet in the public library or in the school library, where will Head Start programs get materials and books without sufficient funds?

Reading parents have reading children. Libraries should foster programs for parents, informational and educational programs to help them "parent"—e.g., how to choose day-care facilities, how to choose educational toys, discussions of quality videos that are available for purchase, computer instruction with their kids, cable TV programs on good books, etc. Consider parent-child learning centers as an alternative approach to programming for preschoolers. The learning centers are special places in the library where parents and children interact together. The tactile experiences, "hands-on" art processes, music, and physical activities are designed to enhance the development of prereading skills and directly involve the parent in the learning process (Rogers & Herrin, 1986, pp. 343-355). The benefits are parent education, service to children, and a positive attitude toward the library.

Other programs and services that reach out into the community are read-a-thons with local bookstores and local celebrities, summer reading programs for which schools loan copies of their books to public libraries for the summer, reading competitions that reward quality reading in liaison with the schools, a holiday activity program on a Saturday for children to allow parents to go shopping without them.

The library should be seen as a focal point of the community, providing service and responding to its needs. A major factor in families is the high percentage of women in the work force. The number of latchkey children has shown a major increase and will continue to rise. There are at least 4 million school age latchkey children in the United States (Hodgkinson, 1985, p. 8). Where are they after school in your community?

Susan Rosenzweig, information manager for the Center for Early Adolescence, has identified criteria for developing responsive after-school programs for young adolescents that are what children and parents want. The successful programs use community resources, invite parent participation, provide staff training, utilize interagency cooperation, and demonstrate longevity in the community. They are proof that energetic and committed adults can meet the challenge of aiding and promoting the healthy development of adolescents (Center for Early Adolescence, 1983, pp. 37-47).

Agencies are part of the community hub. Can your library assist with providing collections of books, provide training to leaders and staff in areas like puppet making and how to share and read a book, or write a newsletter every several months with titles of new preschool books available at the public library?

For teachers and school librarians, how about an annual open house to talk about the best children's books of the year? The books the public librarian is "selling" to kids are the ones the school librarian needs to know since children may be asking for them. If the public librarian prepares a booklist of gift books, it should be sent to the school librarian. Even better, almost every school district has a newsletter that is sent to parents and taxpayers. The school and public librarian should jointly write an article on books to give as gifts to children. Corresponding displays are a good reinforcement. Share your enthusiasm for books by helping teachers bring books into the classroom, helping school librarians keep current with new titles, and helping parents select books to buy with recommended booklists.

These people are paying the taxes that support your library, school or public. Plan your service to benefit them and involve them.

Conclusion

Does all of this sound like you're expected to be six people rolled into one? Yes, it does. The truth of the matter is that the children's librarian and school media specialist are the Renaissance people of the profession. You are expected to know how to run the children's department, know the children's materials both print and nonprint, plan programs, work at the adult reference desk to help cover the schedule (or fill in in the classroom), know the best-sellers and adult reference materials, understand computers and automation, provide outreach to the community, know how to deal with teenagers, have competent managerial skills, often serve as second in command, and smile as you try to cram sixty hours of work into a thirty-five to forty hour work week. Is the adult librarian expected to know children's books? Is a teacher expected to fill in in the school library? Who covers the children's section when you are not there—most likely a page or an aide? Is the director or supervisor expected to have specialist skills as well as administrative ones? The answers are no. Nor is this inequity likely to change.

So how are you supposed to find time to "design" youth services? You make time (remember, youth specialists can do anything). If you don't have a vision of service in mind and goals in sight, your library's service to children is apt to be underfunded, unused, uninviting, or unappreciated.

Hugh Atkinson, in his article "Strategies for Change: Part I," stated: "The prime thing to remember when trying to plan, perform, or simply survive library activities in the next decades is that the value of library successes comes from meeting the needs of the patrons. Those patrons are changing—their attitudes, their economic status, their needs. When our patrons change, then we must change too" (Atkinson, 1984, p 58).

Take a step backward and take a hard look at your current program of service. Use demographics to determine the changes that are shaping your future community, the next decade of children and parents, and the decade after that. What are those changes telling you about the needs of the community?

Stop and look at the pie—plan, implement, and evaluate in terms of these six areas: (1) communication center, (2) reflections—room of mirrors, (3) information retrieval center, (4) library—den—study, (5) energy center, and (6) community hub. Are you in touch; does your image shine; are all avenues of access open to you and the youth you serve; what is your library's role in literacy; is there life, vitality, and energy lighting up your library; and do you know your community and are you involving them in using the library? As long as all of the pieces are in place and aligned with each other, you have a blueprint, a design for service. You are establishing the significance of libraries in an individual's life and the community's existence. The library youth specialist is the Renaissance person of tomorrow. Work from the past, assess the now, design the future.

NOTES

Center for Early Adolescence. (1983). 3-6 p.m.: after-school programming for early adolescence. *Top of the News, 40,* 37-47.

Cummins, J. (1980). Management in children's services. *The Bookmark, 39,* 7-10.

Fasick, A. M. (1984). Moving into the future without losing the past: Children's services in the information age. *Top of the News, 40,* 405-413.

Flagg, G. (1986). In the news: "no adversary," says Bennett. *American Libraries, 17,* 737-739.

Hodgkinson, H. L. (1985). *All one system: Demographics of education-kindergarten through graduate school.* Washington, DC: Institute for Educational Leadership.

Irving, J. (1985). From sheep to shirt: Intergenerational approaches to library programs. *Illinois Libraries, 67,* 82-84.

Lintner, B. (1985). Computers and kids: Capitalizing on a natural compatibility. *Illinois Libraries, 67,* 91-93.

Once upon a time.... (1986). New York: Putnam.

Rogers, P., & Herrin, B. (1986). Parent-child learning centers: An alternative approach to library programming for preschoolers. *Top of the News, 42,* 343-355.

Troutner, J. J. (1983). The magic of interactive video. *Top of the News, 39,* 337-340.

Beckman, M. (1987). Online catalog development at the University of Guelph. *Library Trends, 35,* 527-537.

Florida Center for Library Automation Technical Bulletin. (1986). *1*(5), 3.

Florida, Postsecondary Education Planning Commission. (1988, February 25). *Automation and Networking for Florida Libraries,* p. iv.

Hildreth, C. R. (1987). Beyond Boolean: Designing the next generation of online catalogs. *Library Trends, 35,* 647-667.

Linsley, L. S., et al. (1986). The future is now—the online catalog. *Poster Session, 19.*

Nielson, B., & Baker, B. (1987). Educating the online catalog user: A model evaluation study. *Library Trends, 35,* 571-585.

CHRISTY TYSON

Young Adult Services Coordinator
Spokane Public Library
Spokane, Washington*

Coalition-Building: Maybe Tomorrow? Maybe Today!

It's Tuesday morning at Spokane Public Library. You work your way from the car to the employee's entrance through thirty-five people clutching shopping bags. It's the annual Friends of the Library Used Book Sale. You can get in—they have to wait until nine. They glare. You enter rather more quickly than usual. "Hey, Tyson! Guess what *your kids* were up to last night?" It's the maintenance man. He found the patron sunflower shell stash. You smile and move on not stopping to point out that last week, when they spoke to the city council in support of library funding, they were "our kids." A reference librarian shares the elevator with you. "You've got to do something about those teachers! I've had it with kids who have to read the same book—twenty-five of them last night alone, all looking for some novel that went out of print in 1920." "Yes." you smile. "It's always hard when...." "I don't want sympathy. I want action!"

In the office you reach for the phone. A call to the school is in order, but the director stops by first. "Nice work you did on that budget justification." You begin to bask. "Excellent work for a first draft." The glow fades. "You will have the fleshed-out version in by five, won't you?" Oh well. Who needs lunch? You reach for the phone again, but the first of the young adult selection team drifts in. "I hope you don't expect to see many high school book talks this year. I just can't seem to get in the door." "Well, actually, there are a few other things you could try...." The collection development coordinator leans through the doorway. "Meeting today? Remember if you want the rest of your materials allocation for this year I'll need your order forms by this afternoon." "We're losing money?" chorus the rest of the staff. "But I need more D and D!" "V. C. Andrews!" "Sweet

*Christy Tyson, now Youth Services Consultant with the Alabama Public Library Service, was, at the time of the Allerton Conference, Young Adult Services Coordinator at Spokane (Washington) Public Library.

Valley High!" "Yes, but Nancy here has an interesting problem. How do you get invited to a school if your first contact doesn't work?" "I told her what worked for me. She just didn't want to listen." "Can't we postpone this until next month? I want to order replacements today."

By late afternoon you can breathe a minute. The budget draft is completed. You've submitted your order forms. You've even had a minute to talk with a few young adults who stopped by. You pause. You reach for the phone. The acquisitions clerk brings back your order cards— "Incomplete." Can't call now. It's time to search for missing ISBNs.

You return to your office. The mail has arrived. The phone still waits, but it's really too late to call now. You sort through the mail. Three publisher's catalogs—same company—all addressed to you by name. An invitation to a Planned Parenthood Open House. You'll have to say no. It's the same time as your shift on the reference desk. A newsletter from the regional library association announcing upcoming workshops. Today the one on time management looks especially appealing. You check the dates. You hope the people who attended *last week* enjoyed it. You pause to curse your place on the routing slip. Ah, at last—the latest issue of your favorite library journal. You open the cover, lean back, and freeze as you read the title of the lead article—"Better Living through Coalition-Building." You look at the phone. You hear the voice of your library professor echoing in your memory: "Good outreach is action, not reaction." The line on your job description comes back to haunt you: "Is responsible for interacting regularly with other youth-serving agencies in the community." You gently pound your head against the desk top.

In reality, of course, most days are not quite so overwhelming. I do manage to find time to interact with school personnel, usually through monthly lunches, and to visit most of the youth-serving agencies in the city at least once a year. However, I am all too aware that there is much more that should be done if we are to develop a program that supports the needs and interests of Spokane's young people as fully as they deserve. I also know that even on the most hectic of days I have choices. I would like to think that those choices are based on the library's goals and objectives. However, I know that there are other factors at work for me, and, I suspect, for others in youth services as well. I don't find much value in harangues or breast-beating. Instead, I would like to step back and explore how coalition-building is supported or resisted by the profession.

Coalitions are most commonly defined as groups of agencies, organizations, or individuals with different missions but with some commonality of concerns or interests, coming together to address those areas. Coalitions may be informal—such as the once-a-month lunches in Spokane—or may be highly formalized national or even international groups—such as the Coalition for Literacy or the National Coalition Against Censorship.

Coalitions often lead to more formalized structures such as networks or cooperatives in which contracts are drawn, resources allocated, and missions modified or expanded to reflect the needs of participating agencies as well as the new organization as a whole.

From the earliest days of youth services in American libraries, examples of coalition-building can be found. As early as 1896, when Anne Carroll Moore became head of the Children's Library at Pratt Institute in Brooklyn, the pattern was set. She worked intensively with settlement houses in the area in order to introduce children of the poor to the library despite restrictive policies and protectionist practices of the time. Her work continued through the 1920s at New York Public Library where she is credited with bringing thousands of children into the library, in no small part due to the cooperative relationships she developed with local agencies (Braverman, 1979, pp. 16-72).

In 1906, New York Public Library set another early example of pioneering school-public library interaction. A position was established just to work with schools. Branch libraries were surveyed, resources relegated, staff evaluated, and programs planned to address school-related needs. Through the 1950s this program intensified and expanded to include vocational and parochial schools and also began to include other agencies concerned with youth (Braverman, 1979, pp. 79-113).

In Cleveland, too, the pattern of coalition-building was established early. By the 1940s Jean Roos, administrator of work with youth at Cleveland Public Library, was active on at least twenty youth committees in the area. As at New York Public Library, the connection with local schools was strong, with the public library being responsible for providing school library services in the late 1800s and early 1900s. By the 1920s, the Board of Education had assumed responsibility for providing the quarters for school libraries and for materials that directly related to the curriculum, but the public library shared the cost of salaries and provided support materials, a model of joint planning that continued in one form or another through 1970 (Braverman 1979, pp. 116-177).

Such models are not solitary exceptions or remnants of a bygone era. Indeed, the profession itself has called for and continues to call for coalition-building as part of every library's youth services program. "Young Adult Services in the Public Library" (Public Library Association, American Library Association [ALA], in 1960) and "Standards for Children's Services" (1964) both call for cooperation with schools and other youth-concerned agencies. The first states, "the young adult librarian should maintain contacts with all community agencies serving teenagers and young adults" (Public Library Association, 1960). It goes on to recommend that if a forum for interaction does not exist, the library would do well to take the lead in establishing such a forum. "Standards for

Children's Services in Public Libraries" echoes this recommendation in its Service Objective number 6: "To serve as a social force in the community together with other agencies concerned with the child's welfare" (Public Library Association, 1964). It further advises that this responsibility be extended to the state and national levels as well.

At the state level, an examination of guidelines for youth services in libraries, from those states that have such guidelines, reveals that the call for coalition-building is strong:

—*From Illinois*—"Communication and cooperation with schools and other community agencies serving children should be encouraged and supported" (Illinois Library Association, 1978).

—*From Nebraska*—"The local library must take advantage of the support available from the library system and the state library agency as well as cooperating with school media centers and other community agencies, groups and organizations in planning programs for young people" (Nebraska Library Commission, 1984).

—*From New York*—"Cooperation with other local agencies serving youth and close working relationships with schools are essential for the public library to maintain community awareness....Working with community agencies can help the children's librarian provide better service to children....The children's librarian should establish cooperative relationships with other libraries in the community" (New York Library Association, 1984).

—*From Ohio*—"Cooperation with schools, school media centers and community social service agencies concerned with the welfare of children is encouraged. A sharing and blending of skills, personnel and ideas will benefit all involved" (Ohio Library Association, 1984).

—*From Vermont*—"The public library should serve as a social force in the community by cooperating with other agencies concerned with the child's welfare....libraries should cooperate with other agencies in the community to plan and carry out library-related programs for children. This means the library going into the community as well as groups coming into the library....There is a need for continuous communication between the public library and schools, nursery schools and day care centers in order that all children benefit from the services the public library can provide....A library has the civic responsibility to cooperate with social agenices and institutions involved with education, enrichment and well-being of children in the community" (Vermont Department of Libraries, 1979).

The 1985 American Library Association President's Program theme was "Forging Coalitions for the Public Good." Three of the eight recommendations in "Alliance for Excellence: Librarians Respond to A Nation at Risk" are based on intertype library cooperation. Federal funding in the form of Library Services and Construction Act Title III grants have been allocated just to support interlibrary cooperation. The literature contains many examples of coalition-building, and most of these include a strong call for others to begin or increase their commitment.

Coalition-building is firmly rooted in our professional traditions. Its value is reflected in virtually every document describing youth services from the state or national perspective. Calls for action appear regularly in library literature. Then coalition-building must be an established part of every youth services librarian's work. Yet my experiences in Spokane lead me to believe differently. A 1986 survey conducted in Washington State also indicates that coalition-building is not as widespread as we might assume. Of the sixty-six responding children's and young adult librarians, only twenty-six or 39 percent met with other youth services librarians in their areas to discuss issues and coordinate activities and programs with any regularity at all. Sixty percent had not interacted with other youth services librarians outside their own systems at all during the last year. This disparity between professional expectations and actual experiences demands further consideration. Each of us must ask ourselves: How do I feel about the importance of coalition-building in my work? Is it a high priority? Am I doing as much as I should? Am I doing as much as I would like? Do I enjoy the coalition-building I do? What do I feel are the major obstacles to doing more?

In a 1986 survey, thirty-one children's and young adult services specialists representing twenty-one states were asked similar questions. Some interesting perceptions were revealed. While the majority viewed coalition-building as the third highest priority of their youth services program (following collection development and reference/reader's guidance), 26 percent admitted that they were doing only "so-so" and 42 percent saw themselves as doing "not much of anything" in terms of achieving success (see Appendix 1). It should be noted that, while this perception may seem rather grim, collective assessment of success in outreach is even lower. However, that is another story. For our purposes the pattern is clear. My concerns are not unique. A significant portion of youth services librarians see themselves as doing almost all they should in such in-house, patron-responsive functions as collection development, reader's guidance, and reference, but when they move into more proactive functions such as outreach, programming, and coalition-building, our perceptions of success take a decided dip. We know what we should be doing, but we don't do it. A number of respondents chose to add explanations for low success citing lack of administrative support, uncooperative staff, difficulty of planning for activities outside the library, lack of time, or lack of money. I have no doubt that all these factors play a very large part. They do for me. However, two other factors must also be considered—i.e., perhaps the success level is not in our administrative support but in ourselves.

Even Ferber, a library consultant and specialist in human resource development, lists the following as necessary for effective coalition-building:

> *Interpersonal Communication*, including contacting (establishing rapport), active listening (attentiveness, clarifying, paraphrasing), appropriate *nonverbals* (eye contact, body language).
>
> *Negotiation*, including data gathering, strategizing, probing, blocking attacks, building on others' ideas, acknowledging, constructively criticizing.
>
> *Group Process Facilitation*, including maintenance of group cohesion, getting the task done.
>
> *Assertiveness and Proactive Skills*, including self-initiating, self-directing, self-motivation.
>
> *Networking Skills*, including initiating contacts, convening groups, acting as liaison.
>
> *Problem-Solving*, including brainstorming, problem identification and analysis, action planning.
>
> *Organizational Savvy*, including knowledge of power and influence in the organization through theory, data gathering and analysis.
>
> *A Healthy Self Image*, including good internal sense of worth, appropriate dress and appearance. (Ferber, personal communication, August 13, 1986)

All of these areas—even the last—can be strengthened through training, yet few are included in most library school course offerings. An examination of course listings from fifty-four ALA-accredited master's degree programs revealed that only four offer courses that might support students in the development of any of these skills. Clearly there is a conflict between professional expectations and professional training—at least at the master's degree level. Lack of training cannot help but contribute to the lack of confidence which must impact both our perceived and actual success as coalition builders. We see ourselves as doing very well in the areas most commonly included in library coursework—e.g., collection development and reference/reader's guidance. Respectively, 35 percent and 25 percent felt: "We are doing all we should," and 64 percent and 44 percent gave themselves at least an above-average rating in these areas. However, coalition-building, one of the areas that depends on the kind of skills Ferber describes, was rated as highly successful by only 16 percent of the respondents and moderately successful by an additional 16 percent.

An additional factor that may influence confidence levels in coalition-building is the nature of the organizations with which we interact. Of the forty-one groups with which the ALA's Young Adult Services Division and Association for Library Service to Children have established contact, 37 percent represent human services professions that include interpersonal and organizational skills as part of their training. Not only do we lack the skills we need to operate with full effectiveness in coalition-building, but we also often interact with people who are extremely skilled in just those areas.

Lack of training can be corrected. We can seek out training experiences that will enrich our library education. We can work with local, state, regional, and national groups that support continuing education. We can encourage library schools to offer courses that respond to our needs for behavioral as well as cognitive knowledge.

The second factor that may influence effectiveness as coalition-builders is not a matter of training but of inclination. Comments included in the survey responses suggested a number of reasons why coalition-building was less than successful. However I know that I have used some or all of those reasons to justify not doing things I didn't want to do, and I have managed to do things I really felt were important despite some or occasionally all the factors mentioned by survey respondents. In that typical hectic day described earlier, I made choices to respond to administrative deadlines, to take time to talk with kids, and to open mail. I chose to accept my floorwork schedule as nonnegotiable. I made these decisions and by doing so did not respond to other possibilities including two that would have directly supported coalition-building. Something in me resisted making those actions top priority. It might well have been an almost subconscious response to system goals, but it also might have been personal inclination.

Personal preference—yours and mine—can and does enter into our decision-making processes. It is vital that we know ourselves well enough to detect this influence. The Myers-Briggs Type Indicator is a tool that can be helpful in just this area. Based on Jung's theory of psychological types, it measures perception and judgment—the way we look at things and the way we go about making decisions based on what is perceived. It is, of course, only an indication of tendencies. However, we usually develop more skill with those processes we prefer. We may have a preference for using the right or left hand, but we can and do use either or both when needed. The four areas of preference measured in the Myers-Briggs Type Indicator, then, are:

1. perception directed toward the outer world of people and things (called Extraversion or *E*) or toward the inner world of theories and ideas (Introversion or *I*);
2. perception based on known facts and the directly observable (called Sensing or *S*) or on possibilities and relationships (Intuition or *N*);
3. judgment based on analysis and logic (called Thinking or *T*) or on personal values (Feeling or *F*);
4. judgment in a planned, orderly way (called Judging or *J*) or in a flexible, spontaneous way (Perceptive or *P*) (Myers & McCaulley, 1985, pp. 1-5, 11-29).

While all these factors certainly influence how we approach coalition-building, the first, which considers our preference for perceiving through interaction with people and things rather than through theories and ideas, seems most significant in determining any personal resistance we may have. Myers-Briggs surveyed hundreds of people in a variety of careers and, based on 267 librarians, found a marked preference for introversion—more than 60 percent (Myers & McCaulley, 1985, pp. 244-92). However, since I have heard many of my colleagues express on more than one occasion that youth services specialists may well be more people-oriented than librarians as a whole, I decided to explore this further.

Twelve youth services specialists at Spokane Public Library agreed to take the Myers-Briggs instrument and share the results. Each of us reacted differently to the experience. Most were curious and gained appreciation for ourselves and our colleagues through the process. For some the experience was a real revelation personally as well as professionally. Comments ranged from: "No wonder I get so tired on school visit days!" to "I can't believe it! I finally know why I'm different from the people around me. And it's not because there is something wrong with me!" Now we often describe our actions in terms of the results, as in "Get Marshall to explain this. You're sounding too 'N' for me." We are coming to cherish differences and to capitalize on them.

However, in combination, a clear and somewhat frightening picture emerged. Of the twelve specialists who took the instrument, 75 percent scored in the *I* range, 75 percent in the *N* range, and 75 percent in the *F* range with an equal division between *P* and *J*. At Spokane Public Library, according to the Myers-Briggs results, youth services staff is more concerned with possibilities and relationships than with facts. We base decisions more on personal values than on impersonal analysis and logic. We feel more comfortable in the inner world of theories and ideas than in the outer world of people and things, even more so than librarians in general. No wonder we have such difficulty in coalition-building. Activities based on interaction and dependent on active pursual of contacts are not our preferred styles. Myers-Briggs characterizes the *I* personality by predicting that such people would find work with theories and ideas energizing and work with people and things enervating. However, this insight allows us to do something about it. We can consciously put more energy into those activities we know are not typical of our preferred style. We can acknowledge and turn to those that operate from different styles for strength and support. We can seek out training opportunities that build skills and increase confidence in areas that are not our most preferred. We can continue to explore our own interests, values, and skills so that we will be as aware as possible of the factors that influence our work.

In summary, coalition-building has been a long-standing tradition in library service to youth. It is included as a priority in virtually every set of state and national guidelines. Calls for action are frequent in national forums. Yet our perceptions of success in this area are surprisingly low. Two factors that might affect this have been examined: lack of training in interpersonal and organizational skills; and personality qualities of individual librarians that resist proactive, people-based activities. Yet neither of these factors is insurmountable. Instead, I recommend that as individuals and as a profession we:

—seek out training experiences in interpersonal and organizational skills to supplement library school education;

—actively work for continuing education experiences at the local, state, and national levels that enhance these skills;

—work for more responsive library school curricula;

—reconsider recruitment of library school students;

—encourage library systems to provide for human resource development training and support; and

—accept the challenge of self-knowledge and learn to value the differences in attitudes, values, and skills of our colleagues.

More research is necessary in both issues discussed in this presentation. My inquiries were limited and basic, but the tendencies uncovered have significance for current and projected training and exploration. Who we are as real or potential coalition-builders is not solely determined by who we claim to be in policies and guidelines. We are also formed by our training and by our own natures. In Spokane we have begun to learn more about who we are and how we act and interact in order to increase our effectiveness at work. We have made a commitment to continue this exploration. However we must all commit as individuals and as a profession to honest consideration of how differences in skills and personalities impact our actions. When this happens, I predict the next survey that comes our way will be marked: "We are doing all we should."

APPENDIX

Summary of a 1986 Survey of Youth Services Managers

August 18, 1986

Dear Colleague,

In preparing a presentation for the upcoming Allerton Institute I am looking into youth services managers' attitudes toward delivery of service. This is nothing scientific at this point. I am curious only about general trends that might exist. Please take a minute to mark the following scales and send me your responses by August 31. A self-addressed envelope is enclosed for your use. Remember I'm looking for your impressions as to how well your system is doing. All responses will be kept confidential. THANK YOU FOR YOUR COOPERATION!

Christy Tyson
Spokane Public Library

----

1. Our system gives collection development for youth

/ 45%	3%	/ 29%	10%	13% /
high		medium		low

2. Our system gives reader's guidance/reference to youth

/ 25%	19%	/ 28%	9%	19% /

3. Our system gives in-house programming to youth

/ 21%	6%	/ 17%	6%	50% /

4. Our system gives coalition-building with other youth-serving agencies

/ 23%	13%	/ 23%	10%	32% /

5. Our system gives outreach to youth (booktalks, school visits, etc.)

/ 26%	13%	/ 16%	3%	42% /

6. In the area of COALITION-BUILDING,

/ 16%	16%	/ 26%	0%	42% /
We are doing all we should.		so-so		We aren't doing much of anything.

7. In the area of COLLECTION DEVELOPMENT,

/ 35%	29%	/ 19%	3%	13% /

8. In the area of IN-HOUSE PROGRAMMING,

/ 19%	19%	/ 16%	10%	35% /

9. In the area of OUTREACH,

/ 10%	23%	/ 23%	6%	39% /

10. In the area of REFERENCE/READER'S GUIDANCE,

/ 25%	19%	/ 34%	3%	19% /

50 surveys sent to 25 different states
31 responses from 21 different states

NOTES

Braverman, M. (1979). *Youth, society, and the public library.* Chicago: ALA.

Illinois Library Association, Children's Librarians' Section, Ad Hoc Committee on Standards for Children's Library Service. (1978). *Guidelines for public library service to children.* Pamphlet, Illinois Library Association, Springfield.

Myers, I. B., & McCaulley, M. H. (1985). *Manual, a guide to the development and use of the Myers-Briggs type indicator.* Palo Alto, CA: Consulting Psychologists Press.

Nebraska Library Commission. (1984). *Guidelines for young people's library service in Nebraska.* Pamphlet (draft), Nebraska Library Commission, Lincoln.

New York Library Association, Youth Services Section. Task Force on Standards for Youth Services. (1984). *Standards for youth services in public libraries of New York State.* Pamphlet, New York Library Association, New York.

Ohio Library Association, Children's Services in Libraries and School Media Centers Division. (1984). *A guideline to planning public library service to children in Ohio.* Pamphlet, Ohio Library Association, Columbus.

Public Library Association, Committee on Standards for Work with Young Adults. (1960). *Young adult services in the public library.* Pamphlet, American Library Association, Chicago.

Public Library Association, Subcommittee on Standards for Children's Services. (1964). *Standards for children's services in public libraries.* Pamphlet, American Library Association, Chicago.

Vermont Department of Libraries, Task Force on Children's Services. (1979). *Recommendations for public library service to children in Vermont.* Pamphlet, Vermont Department of Libraries, Montpelier.

Washington Library Association, Children's and Young Adult Services, Steering Committee for State Guidelines of Youth Services in Public Libraries of Washington State. (1986). *Survey of children's and young adult services.* Survey, Washington Library Association, Olympia.

ADDITIONAL READING

Wilson, E. (1983). The librarian in the youth services network: Nationally and locally. In E. V. LiBretto (Ed.), *New Directions for young adult services* (pp. 103-15). New York: R. R. Bowker.

Notes on Coalitions

Allen, P. R. (1983). Toward meeting the information needs of young people in New York City. In E. V. LiBretto (Ed.), *New directions for young adult services* (pp. 117-28). New York: R. R. Bowker.

Blake, F. M., et al. (1985, July). *Forging coalitions for the public good.* Paper presented at the American Library Association President's Program, Chicago.

Henington, D. M. (1986). Cooperation in serving students. In A. Ladenson (Ed.), *The urban public library makes connections for better service* (pp. 17-25). Chicago: Urban Libraries Council.

Howard, E. N. (1978). Local power and the community library. *Public Library Reporter, 18.*

Miller, S. M. (1983, Fall). Coalition etiquette: Ground rules for building coalitions. *Social Policy,* p. 19.

Rosenzweig, S. (1986). Libraries and liaisons: Expanding the network. *Top of the News 42* (4), 367-374.

Sullivan, P. A. (1979). Library cooperation to serve youth. In J. V. Rogers (Ed.), *Libraries and young adults* (pp. 113-18). Littleton, CO: Libraries Unlimited, Inc.

Notes on Interpersonal
and Organizational Exploration

Forydyce, J. K., & Weil, R. (1979). *Managing with people: A manager's handbook of organiza-tion development methods*. Reading, MA: Addison-Wesley.

Hampden-Turner, C. (1982). *Maps of the mind*. New York: Macmillan.

Johnston, D. W., and Johnson, F. P. (1975). *Joining together: Group therapy and group skills*. Englewood Cliffs, NJ: Prentice-Hall, Inc.

Miller, S., et al. (1981). *Straight talk: A new way to get closer to others by saying what you really mean*. New York: Rawson, Wade Publishing, Inc.

Powell, J. W., & LeLieuvre, R. B. (1979). *Peoplework. Communications dynamics for librar-ians*. Chicago: American Library Association.

FRANCES M. McDONALD

Associate Professor
Library Media Education
Mankato State University
Mankato, Minnesota

Access to Information: Professional Responsibility and Personal Response

The library community devotes much attention to outsiders who attempt to impose their views on the collection development process. The library community expects that insiders will rally and, with profound indignation, resist efforts by outsiders to censor library resources. Actual happenings illustrate that this does not always occur. In fact, well-publicized challenges seem to result in restrictive practices by some librarians.

A school librarian declares that she will not purchase a Judy Blume book because Blume's books cause too much trouble (Hentoff, 1983, p. vii). A secondary school librarian states that "we are somewhat selective in our choice of library resources" (McDonald, 1983, p. 10). A public librarian, after a successful young adult Dungeons and Dragons program, vows not to repeat the program because of isolated community reaction.

There is no indignation at these events, just understanding. There is no outcry, just a recognition that the librarian was acting to survive and that it could easily have been any librarian. The rationale for these actions explains the difference between the motivations of the outsiders and the motivations of the librarians. They say: "I disapprove of the ideas in this book." Librarians say, "the book has no literary merit," or "my budget has been cut and I can't buy everything." The outsiders mean that they fear the ideas in the book. Librarians mean that they fear the results to themselves, and they fear the outsiders.

While virtually all of the voluminous writing on censorship focuses on the actions of outsiders, much of the actual censorship is done by librarians. Quietly, under the guise of selection, spurred by rumors of controversy, or the tainting of an author because of continuous efforts to remove her books, a librarian removes a book, creates a restricted shelf, or neglects to buy a potentially controversial title.

These incidents are not publicized; they never reach the collective consciousness. Librarians do not report their self-censorship to the press.

In effect, librarians erect more barriers to information in their day-to-day activities than are imposed from the outside. Persons in the library community need to examine their reasoning and beliefs and face the fact that the most serious threat to access to information comes not from those outside but, in fact, results from the fears, values, and actions of librarians.

The library community has known that librarians have censored materials since the fifties and sixties when Fiske (1959) and Farley (1964) reported their research. During the 1970s, Busha (1972) affirmed earlier findings and added significant information about the characteristics of librarians who exhibit censorious inclinations. Pope (1974) and Woods and Salvatore (1981) provided more evidence that librarians are not purists in defending intellectual freedom. Recently, Hopkins (1984, pp. 9-22) reported a trend toward more self-censorship by librarians. The formerly secret plague of librarians—self-censorship, safe selection, restricted circulation—is out of the closet.

Hopkins (1984) asked: "How widespread is precensorship by library media specialists and what can the profession do about it at whatever level" (p. 18)? This presentation represents one person's answer to that question. It is time for the profession of librarianship to stop focusing on challenges to resources and begin to examine why knowledge of intellectual freedom, as expressed in the Library Bill of Rights and the Interpretations, is not enough to ensure that librarians will uphold freedom-to-read principles. Why do librarians who subscribe to a Code of Ethics (American Library Association, 1985-1986, p. 226), violate its principles? Why do librarians who know the value of selection policies and procedures, fail to follow them? The library profession must examine why librarians are able to articulate the values of the profession and yet act contrary to those values. Is it the preparation programs? Is it personal characteristics, levels of adult development, or the cognitive development of librarians? Is it a combination of factors?

> The commitment to the public's right to read must go beyond the verbalization stage where many librarians readily give lip service to the library user's right to inquiry. A true commitment to freedom of access to books and information should progress from the realm of abstract conceptualization to functional operation in the day-to-day activities of the librarian, especially when a library is confronted with censorship pressures. (Busha, 1972, p. 4)

Based on observations of current professional practice and the limited research available, it is possible to speculate about what factors affect the inclination of librarians to act in a manner consistent with principles of freedom to read. Three personal components appear to influence reactions to censorship pressures: first, personal characteristics of the librarian; second, level of commitment to a professional ethic; and third, the professional preparation of the librarian. Three external components appear to shape the personal components: first the milieu in which the librarian works—institutional expectations, the authority and management style of supervisors, and the characteristics and professional commitment of coworkers; second, actual community response to access to information, including press reactions to First Amendment freedoms for children and young adults; and third, perceptions of community values and likely tolerance of intellectual freedom. This presentation focuses on the personal components.

Personal Characteristics

Librarians talk about censorship as something being done to them. They identify the censor as the irate parent who calls the principal, or stops at the office of the head librarian, or contacts the library trustee. However, definitions of censorship make it clear that government authorities or their agents are the censors, not parents or other citizens. In spite of Fiske's (1959), Farley's (1964), and Busha's (1972) findings, librarians refuse to accept the term for themselves. Librarians compromise, librarians hold procensorship attitudes, and librarians censor. Yet librarians profess belief in the intellectual freedom principles in the Library Bill of Rights.

Downs (1984) speculated that perhaps there was something in the psychological makeup or personality of librarians which led to their differing approaches to the selection and restriction of library resources (p. 8). Discussing parental reactions to young adult books, but applicable in the context of the librarian as censor, Broderick (1984) said "it is unclear (because we have no real psychological research into the characteristics of censors) whether the censors have never achieved the *formal operations* stage in their cognitive development or do not understand the process that must be gone through to achieve this level of thought" (p. 44). Fiske (1959) concluded that school and public librarians do not feel strongly enough "as individuals or as professionals to assert" intellectual freedom values in the "face of public disapproval" (p. 110). Busha (1972) showed a correlation between authoritarian beliefs and procensorship attitudes in public librarians (p. 336). Farley (1964) found that more than half of the secondary school librarians interviewed expressed "weak, wavering, uncertain, or contradictory" (p. 122) attitudes toward library censorship and concluded that "librarians censor books because of a *pressure* which they cannot identify" (emphasis added) (p. 325).

> It may be suggested by this research. . .that the school librarian who contemplates the censoring of a book against his better judgment and because of "pressure" has a professional obligation to take thought and to attempt to identify this pressure to his own satisfaction, if indeed any real pressure actually exists. (p. 335)

Donelson (1981) said: "I have no idea how many people preach freedom and education while stocking only those books that please the community, placate the censor, ignore modern problems, eschew moral issues, and therefore avoid controversies" (p. 12). The Office for Intellectual Freedom (1983) described four factors which motivate the censor—family values, political views, religion, and minority rights—and added that no citizen and no librarian can properly assume the duty or right to restrict or suppress legally protected expressions of ideas (pp. 173-74).

The library profession does not know the characteristics of a librarian who firmly espouses and practices intellectual freedom principles. Also, the profession does not know whether librarians, who successfully resist efforts to restrict information, exhibit similar characteristics. The profession does not know what life stages or passages lead to the ability to comprehend the concepts of intellectual freedom. It is not as simple as age and experience. These qualities do not guarantee upholding the Library Bill of Rights or only first- or second-year librarians would be practicing self-censorship. We know that this is not the case.

Professional Ethics

The next component influencing the librarian's reaction to censorship pressures is the librarian's level of commitment to a professional ethic. Behavior in a challenge situation or a self-censorship situation cannot be predicted from a librarian's verbal report of valuing an ethical standard. People who travel around the country speaking to librarians about intellectual freedom issues report instances of rapt audiences, nodding in agreement at every intellectual freedom platitude uttered, with apparent understanding and acceptance of the principles being expounded. But, invariably, the first remarks following the presentation illustrate that librarians are able to justify self-censorship by the unique conditions in which they work. "Everything you say is right, but I live in a conservative community (or state)," or, "my principal has said I must keep the community in mind when I select." Nat Hentoff illustrates the point with descriptions of the personal reactions of several librarians. Two Minnesota librarians told Hentoff they would not order Judy Blume books because her books are " 'too much trouble' to have in a library." An Illinois high school librarian, convinced that abortion is murder, will have no books "that may...encourage students to commit murder." In Massachusetts, there will be no antiabortion books because a school official is convinced that these books promote religion (Hentoff, 1983, p. vii).

Reading a Code of Ethics or the Library Bill of Rights does not tell the librarian how to apply the principles contained in the documents. Deciding what to do, while balancing conflicting claims and loyalties, marks the application of a Code of Ethics. Fully subscribing to the Code of Ethics means librarians need to be active in shaping the world in which they work and not remain passive and be molded by it. If the people the librarian works with do not understand freedom to read concepts, the librarian will experience great difficulty in exercising ethical behavior. Confronted with conditions in the workplace antithetical to intellectual freedom, the librarian can work to change those conditions or reject the ethics of the profession and compromise. Rather than accepting the view of the principal, the library trustee, or the vocal citizen, the librarian has a professional responsibility to proselytize about the only issue on which there are no opposing viewpoints. If librarians do not explain, exhort, and teach the importance of the principles governing librarianship, who will do it?

Professional Preparation of Librarians

The third component which shapes the personal responses of librarians is their professional preparation. No one disputes the fact that intellectual freedom receives attention during library school. Students in library media education courses spend considerable time studying the principles of selection. Students learn to develop and apply criteria for the selection of resources. Librarians are taught the importance of following approved policies and procedures when resources are challenged. Freedom of access to information is promoted as a professional value. However, in spite of passing tests on principles of selection, writing drafts of selection policies, and being able to apply valid criteria to the selection of resources, librarians' professional practices do not always reflect what was learned. Library educators appear to believe that if students are presented with a Library Bill of Rights during their professional preparation, they will have learned what it means and will transfer its principles to behavior at the reference desk, the circulation desk, or when selecting resources. Apparently library media educators expect that if cognitive objectives are met, there will be a corresponding development of appropriate behavior. The expectation is unfounded because self-censorship suggests that library education has not been effective in teaching students to apply the Library Bill of Rights in the workplace.

The Proposed Agenda

Solving the problem of the conflict between professional responsibility and personal reactions requires efforts on the part of the entire library profession including library media educators, professional organizations, and librarians themselves. A threefold agenda is being proposed: first, an education which includes affective development as well as cognitive development; second, a profession willing to work to foster community understanding of the First Amendment and the principles of freedom to read and to create a climate of intellectual freedom among the persons with whom the librarian works—e.g., supervisors, teachers, administrators, library trustees, and school board members; and third, a research agenda to identify the factors which contribute to the willingness or reluctance of librarians to act on intellectual freedom principles.

Library Education

Clearly, an entrance requirement that incoming students demonstrate the right personal characteristics before admittance to library school is not being suggested. Granted, the task would be easy if all students arrived with an understanding of the First Amendment learned in eighth grade civics class. They do not. The suspected amount of self-censorship indicates that current teaching strategies have been unsuccessful in helping librarians apply freedom to read principles. Library media educators must examine current methods and revise them. Library school faculty must develop learning strategies designed to help students learn to transfer the principles of the First Amendment to professional library practice.

Educators are beginning to understand how to accomplish the type of learning needed to prepare library media specialists who are willing to act on their expressed beliefs. Educational psychologists tell us that there are three domains in the learning environment—cognitive, affective, and psychomotor. Since the psychomotor domain deals with physical skills, it does not apply here. The cognitive domain represents information—i.e., knowing the norms of the group. The affective domain concentrates on attitudes and values, which lead to behavior consistent with the norms of the profession (Bloom, 1956; Krathwol et al., 1964). Both knowing and valuing are essential to create First Amendment activists.

Library education, as most of education, emphasizes knowing, specifically the lower levels of cognitive learning. But cognition goes beyond knowing and comprehending, to what are commonly called higher order thinking skills—application, analysis, synthesis, and evaluation. It is these higher thinking skills that will provide the librarian with the ability to analyze actions, to consider the implications of actions, to weigh competing values, and to make judgments consistent with the values of the profession. Educational activities designed to help students apply and evaluate intellectual freedom principles in the context of professional practice might help librarians transfer knowledge to the workplace. However, educating the mind and hoping that appropriate behavior will follow is not enough.

Behavior has a cognitive component and an affective component. Learning about intellectual freedom will only lead to action if the student has an opportunity to participate in activities also emphasizing affective learning. Affective learning begins with awareness, moves to attitudes and valuing and, if effective, results in actions. Library education must not merely focus on attitudes in the abstract but must present concrete situations, real and simulated, to help students examine how committed they are to their expressed values and how their values must translate to behavior. When actions do not reflect stated values, the librarian rationalizes in terms of competing values in an attempt to explain the discrepancy. Library students need to have an opportunity to analyze these competing pressures and examine the implications of actions. While raising awareness alone will not change attitudes or values, creating dissonance by allowing students to experience the conflict between theory and practice does contribute to a clarification of values and might prepare students to respond to the pressures they will face. The cognitive and affective components in a response to a censorship incident or an inclination to self-censorship are illustrated in Table 1.

The message for library educators goes beyond what has been proposed in curriculum reform. Library school faculty must also model intellectual freedom behavior and activism. All facets of professional preparation must be couched in the spirit of intellectual freedom. Selection courses are not the only place where principles of intellectual freedom are taught. Discussions in reference, administration, cataloging, and other courses must illustrate practices that enhance or create barriers to access information. A total library school curriculum, viewed as the forum for the education of intellectual freedom activists, enhances the likelihood of success.

TABLE 1
PROCESS OF RESPONSE TO INTELLECTUAL FREEDOM INCIDENT

Component	*Cognitive*	*Affective*
Perceiving of a censorship situation including recognition of how actions might affect others.	Information Knowledge	Awareness
Integrating of various considerations in order to formulate what course of action would best fulfill an ethical ideal.	Reasoning Comprehension	Responding
Deciding, calculating, weighing, and considering other values.	Analysis Synthesis	Valuing
Implementing and executing a plan of action, evaluating competence, and expected difficulties.	Evaluation	Acting

Adapted from: Rest, J. R. (1984). The major components of morality. In W. M. Kurtines & J. L. Gewirtz (Eds.), *Morality, moral behavior, and moral development* (pp. 24-38). New York: John Wiley.

Creating a Climate of Intellectual Freedom

Efforts of library school faculty will not accomplish all that is needed. Librarians do not work in a vacuum. The institution in which they work provides one key to whether librarians will act on their intellectual freedom beliefs. Many librarians find themselves working in hostile environments where avoiding controversy and compromise are the predominant values. Creating an intellectual freedom climate under these circumstances presents difficulties. The concepts of intellectual freedom must be translated to institutional values for teachers, administrators, and city and county officials. Skills of persuasion will enable librarians to counter the censoring efforts of coworkers, supervisors, and the community. Members of governing boards need orientation to understand the importance of protecting access to information. The library profession, through public education, lobbying, and forming coalitions with other groups, needs to participate in fostering a climate in which access to information will flourish and individual librarians will feel secure in acting on their professional values and beliefs.

Professional Organizations

Professional organizations share the responsibility for promoting a climate of intellectual freedom and for the continuing professional development of their members. Programming that focuses on exchanging information about the evils the censors are doing will not accomplish the task. In fact, librarians might be frightened into increased self-censorship with this information. Programming at professional meetings must focus on the attitudes and behavior of librarians. Exercises like the ones provided by YASD (Young Adult Services Division) and AASL (American Association of School Libraries) force librarians to examine their practices in the light of association policy. This consciousness raising might cause some librarians to reexamine their commitment to intellectual freedom (American Library Association, 1982; American Library Association, 1986). Programs featuring case histories demonstrate how censorship pressures can be resisted and provide encouragement to wavering and uncertain librarians. Professional organizations contribute to the continuing education of their members by providing opportunities to acquire and sharpen skills. Librarians do not need to hear about numbers and the titles that have been censored, but they do need to practice skills and see examples of successful resistance to censorship efforts.

Research

Current research only hints at factors contributing to the discrepancy between professional beliefs and professional practices. The library profession needs to examine studies that have been completed and verify or reject the findings. Do the personal characteristics of individual librarians determine their responses to censorship pressures? Is it authoritarian beliefs as Busha hinted? Is it lack of commitment to a professional ethic as Fiske charged? Is it a personal belief system as Hentoff illustrated? Is it something in the personality or psychological makeup of librarians as Downs speculated? Is it personal values as Krug intimated? Or, is it lack of cognitive development as Broderick suggested? Or is it none of these factors but some as yet unknown variable? Ignoring the hints will not solve the problem, but continued investigation might. Research could provide a scientific base for curriculum revision, for continuing education activities, and for a professional plan to eliminate the self-censorship that seems so pervasive.

Conclusion

The task is formidable, but supporters of the First Amendment number in the millions. The library profession must identify its allies, enlist their aid, and launch a massive intellectual freedom effort. This effort could provide librarians with a sense of community as well as professional support thereby encouraging integrity in selection and access decisions. Further, librarians must assume personal responsibility for their professional practices. They must stop using real or assumed outside pressures to excuse or to avoid facing their violations of professional ethics. Librarians must consciously examine the values that lead to restrictive library practices. Through library media education, continuing education, and programming at professional meetings, it is possible to create generations of intellectual freedom missionaries courageous enough to act on the belief system they all profess. Only this will ensure information access for children and young adults.

NOTES

American Library Association. (1985-1986). On professional ethics. In *ALA Policy Manual* (p. 226). Chicago, IL: ALA.

American Library Association. American Association of School Librarians. (1986). *Intellectual freedom and censorship: Do school practices reflect association policy?* Unpublished questionnaire, American Library Association, American Association of School Librarians, Chicago.

American Library Association. Office for Intellectual Freedom. (1983). *Intellectual freedom manual.* Chicago, IL: ALA.

American Library Association. Young Adult Services Division. (1982). *Does your library violate the library bill of rights...and not know it?* Unpublished questionnaire, American Library Association, Young Adult Services Division, Chicago.

Bloom, B., et al. (1956). *Taxonomy of educational objectives.* New York: David McKay.

Broderick, D. M. (1983). Adolescent development and censorship. In *School library media annual* (Vol. 1, p. 6). Littleton, CO.

Busha, C. H. (1972). *Freedom versus suppression and censorship: With a study of the attitudes of midwestern public librarians and a bibliography of censorship.* Littleton, CO: Libraries Unlimited.

Donelson, K. L. Shoddy and pernicious books and youthful purity: Literacy and moral censorship, then and now. *Library Quarterly, 51,* 12.

Downs, R. B. (1984). *The first freedom today: Critical issues relating to censorship and intellectual freedom.* Chicago, IL: ALA.

Farley, J. J. (1964). *Book censorship in the senior high school libraries of Nassau County, New York.* Unpublished doctoral dissertation, New York University.

Fiske, M. (1959). *Book selection and censorship: A study of school and public libraries in California.* Berkeley, CA: University of California Press.

Hentoff, N. (1983). Foreword. In H. Bosmajian (Ed.), *Censorship, libraries, and the law.* New York: Neal-Schuman.

Hopkins, D. M. (1984). Censorship of school library media materials and its implications, 1982-1983. In S. Aaron & P. R. Scales (Eds.), *School library media annual 1984* (Vol. 2, pp. 9-22). Littleton, CO: Libraries Unlimited.

Krathwol, D. R., et al. (1964). *Taxonomy of educational objectives.* New York: David McKay.

McDonald, F. (1983). *A report of a survey on censorship in public elementary and high school libraries and public libraries in Minnesota.* Minneapolis, MN: Civil Liberties Union.

Pope, M. (1974). *Sex and the undecided librarian: A study of librarian's opinions on sexually oriented literature.* Metuchen, NJ: Scarecrow Press.

Rest, J. R. (1984). The major components of morality. In W. M. Kurtines & J. L. Gewirtz (Eds.), *Morality, moral behavior, and moral development* (pp. 24-28). New York: John Wiley.

Woods, L. B., & Salvatore, L. (Winter, 1981). Self-censorship in collection development by high school library media specialists. *School Media Quarterly 9,* 102-108.

SUSAN ROSENZWEIG

Information Manager
Center for Early Adolescence
Chapel Hill, North Carolina

Part I: Funding for Youth Services— How to Do It and Where to Find It

No one ever said that part of the job of a young adult librarian would be fund-raising. I took all the courses needed to best serve young people—but mention was never made in any course, by any teacher, of how one goes about getting funding for programs and materials that are not included in the regular library budget. Nor did anyone ever suggest that, in fact, that is part of a librarian's job. Evidently no one predicted that it would be necessary. So why is it a special issues session at this institute?

It seems that most children's and young adult librarians had an experience similar to mine. One children's coordinator reported that the branch children's librarians do not think about fund-raising for special projects—they do not come to her with requests, do not see it as one of their jobs, and are afraid to ask for money. After all, the library is a public institution supported by tax dollars, how can they ask for more money? And they are so timid about asking for money, that when they do ask, it is for minimal amounts.

Yet in this age of tight funding and increased competition for what is available—from government sources as well as from foundations and individuals—we must be competitive in order to get enough of the share of the pie to carry out the services necessary to fulfill the mission of young adult librarian. If we don't, we will be reduced to providing minimum services with inadequate resources. And if we are willing to settle for that, what will that do for the entire field of children's and young adult librarianship, and ultimately to the young people we serve?

This discussion will begin with a review of the fundamentals of grantsmanship, and you will find that these are basic tasks that need to be accomplished to promote children's or young adult library service under any circumstances. This will be followed by suggestions for how to get a bigger piece of the existing budget; how to obtain funding from corporations, foundations, individuals, and other sources; and what kinds of nonmonetary contributions should be considered. Applying for LSCA monies will be discussed in part II. This will not be a "how to write a proposal" approach. Not that it isn't important to know such techniques, but there are many excellent resources available to help with the nuts and bolts of the process. The focus here will be on the broader issues and will be touching on the very basic question of what does a children's or young adult librarian do, or rather, what *should* he or she be doing?

Preparation for this presentation included interviews with direct services librarians, age-level coordinators, and state library directors in small, medium, and large library systems. I talked to people for whom getting money was a major part of their jobs and to others who did it on their own. The people interviewed are very successful at getting contributions, both monetary and in-kind. They were asked how they do it? What is the bureaucracy involved? What advice would they offer for successful fund-raising, and what they would like to hear at a conference like this. They were also asked to share their successes and failures. Their answers, and what was found in the literature frame my discussion.

There is no question that fund-raising has not traditionally been considered part of the job. A literature and database search yielded very few books and articles that were specifically addressed to librarians. There are scores of publications on fund-raising, marketing, and public relations in general, but in the few that do address librarians, almost nothing is said about school librarians. There is some promising news on the horizon. A new periodical, *The Bottom Line: A Financial Magazine for Librarians* is now available, and a new book from Greenwood Press, *Grant Proposal Writing: A Handbook for School Library Media Specialists,* has recently been published. The ALSC Grants Committee is also compiling a list of national foundations that can be tapped for funds.

For survival's sake, children's and young adult librarians must take a broader view of their profession. They must add to their job descriptions fund-raising, marketing, and public relations. The following "laundry list" of basics offers nothing that is earthshakingly new—but they are included here because they are essential for success in getting support. The list includes doing your homework, knowing the research, having an evaluation component, being politically savvy, marketing services, doing public relations, knowing the organizational structure of the library or school, knowing the institutional mission, and having clear goals and objectives.

Doing your homework is very important. An analysis of the community that is served by the library is fundamental in order to ascertain its needs. This includes the statistical data—e.g., total population of the community; the number of children and young adults; projected growth or decline of the age group served; ethnic composition; educational levels of the population; school enrollment; and economic factors such as income, occupations, etc. Add information about social and service organizations in the community, the transportation system, communications network, political makeup, and other available information sources. Information can be gleaned from other quarters one might not ordinarily think of such as the police, the Chamber of Commerce, bartenders, crossing guards, church records, immigration records, mailmen, retired people, Welcome Wagon, voter registration, youth clubs, and undertakers. It is necessary to know how many working parents there are in both single and dual-career families. Knowing the community is essential for fund-raising, and it is even more crucial for determining the services that will meet the needs of the population served.

Doing your homework also includes knowing how your institution works. Who should be approached when you want additional materials or money to do a new program, and what is the procedure? In a very small system this may be very informal, consisting of an oral request of the director. In larger systems there is likely to be a more formal procedure that would involve moving up the hierarchy—beginning with a request to the branch head, then to a coordinator or age-level consultant, and then to the deputy director where the ultimate decision is made. If the request is for a substantial amount, a final step might be approved by the board of trustees. Every system has its own procedure and knowing what the procedure is, is essential.

Before you even think about approaching anyone with a request, have a clear idea of what you want the money for. Can a need be demonstrated and documented for this program or service? Will it address a problem in the community? Are goals clear? Can you demonstrate that the project has validity and appeal? Is it compatible with the mission of the larger institution? Has every item been costed out including staff time, postage, materials, duplicating, and so forth?

Being aware of any research that will support a request will help enormously. For example, if additional money is needed for a summer reading program, citing Barbara Heyns's study on the positive effects of summer learning on school achievement is certain to strengthen your position. Heyns (1978) states: "The single summer activity that is most strongly and consistently related to summer learning is reading" (p. 161). She goes on to argue that the one institution that directly influences children's reading is the public library (p. 161). This cannot fail to be persuasive given current concern about literacy levels and school dropouts.

If you have been successful in funding this project before and you want to repeat or continue it, offering proof of its success will be critical. Make sure an evaluation component is built into every program or service provided. Document what you have done and use the data collected to justify the request.

Know how to market your services, do public relations, sharpen networking skills, and be politically knowledgeable about the community. These are the "final four" for successful fund-raising. They are probably obvious but are not always tended to. Make sure that people know what you are doing both within the library or school system and out in the community. Good public relations and marketing not only attract children and young adults to your program, but also enhance the chances that bond issues and referenda will be approved by the voting public and increase the likelihood that special projects will be funded. Networking and being politically savvy fall under the category of "people skills." Know the people who serve on the school board, the library board, bank officers, and Friends of the Library. Become a member of the Chamber of Commerce, the local United Way, or any other organization that involves important people in the community. For school librarians, cultivate your staff, principal, and PTA. Make sure it is known what the other youth-serving agencies in the community are doing and who the people are who work in them. This quotation sums up the importance of people skills. " 'You will not raise a dime until you raise a friend' " (Waters, 1986, p. 37).

To all of this add a dose of creativity and initiative and you are ready to continue the process. All of this is a tall order. Be reassured, however, that none of the earlier mentioned can be accomplished quickly or easily. Fund-raising takes time, patience, and perseverance, and it is hard work. The art of cultivating people is just that—an art (as is fund-raising)—that cannot be created instantaneously. And although it could be argued that all of us need to be tending to these basic tasks as professionals, not every school media specialist, children's or young adult librarian is cut out to be a fund-raiser. As the manager of children's services for the Louisville Public Library pointed out: "Fundraising is difficult. Not everyone is good at it" (Somerville, personal communication, October 24, 1986). If you are interested in fund-raising but feel that you do not know enough to do it, there are many workshops available that teach fund-raising techniques. These range from one day to five days in length and represent a fairly modest investment considering the return. Alternatives to finding the money yourself are turning to the grants coordinator in your system—if you are lucky enough to have one—or asking for help from a staff member who has been successful at fund-raising.

Combining fund-raising efforts with those for other services is also a possibility. The Louisville Public Library received an H. W. Wilson award to improve relations with patrons. Included in their application was improving relations with child and young adult patrons. By the way, it is probably easier to get funding for children's services than anything else. According to Barb Fierro, former executive director of Girls Club of Rapid City, South Dakota: "Children's needs tug at everyone's heart strings"

(Fierro, personal communication, October 27, 1986). These are the basic principles underlying successful fund-raising, and successful librarianship.

The discussion will now move to the types of funding that are available to librarians, beginning closest to home and ending with a discussion in Part II of federal grants.

Examine first the opportunities within your system for either getting a bigger piece of the budget pie, or finding funding outside the regular budget. Whether you work in a small or large system, be familiar with the budget process—i.e., the size of the budget and how it is allocated. The process for requesting a larger share will vary from system to system. In the New York Public Library, for example, the materials budget is based on level of circulation and how well the money was spent in the prior budget period. Careful documentation and data collection might enable a direct services librarian to increase his or her share of funds. In addition, the New York Public Library has special funds in the young adult and children's budget. Very active age-level specialists in the borough of Queens see to it that their librarians get some of these funds to promote special services and programs. In this situation, the age-level specialists depend on the direct services librarian to approach them with project plans.

According to Barbara Elleman (1986), editor of children's books for *Booklist,* for school libraries, "[t]he principal is the link to the purse strings." She gives helpful advice to school principals in an issue of *Here's How* on how to vitalize the school library. School librarians can turn her advice to their own advantage.

Other sources are available within one's system—e.g., Friends of the Library, the PTA, and patrons themselves. In 1985, $28 million was raised by Friends groups across the country (Margolis, 1986, p. 7). One group held a Thanksgiving pie sale and raised enough money to buy new furniture, toys, and VCRs and to offer community cooking classes. Book sales run by Friends' groups and PTAs can raise thousands of dollars for a library. Want a piece of that pie? Know how the money is allocated, and know the people who have decision-making power. And last, but certainly not least, tap the young people in your system.

In the Virginia Beach Public Library, teenagers raised money for the programs they wanted. What a great way to involve the community and publicize services while at the same time giving young people an opportunity for meaningful participation in the community.

After you have exhausted all the possibilities of getting money from within your institution and you still need funds, where do you turn next? The next step should be local sources of funding.

These include local businesses and merchants, local foundations and corporations, your local United Way, and individuals. When approaching local businesses and corporations, the key to remember is that "people give because they 'get something' out of giving" (Brakely, 1986, p. 26). The "something" they get need not be tangible. They may get a good feeling from giving, they may give to feel wanted and appreciated, or because they believe in the cause. Guilt may be the motivating factor, or a desire for power and influence. And don't overlook the part peer pressure plays, or the competitive spirit. What you must do is correctly assess the person you are approaching. Is he or she the type that is big-hearted, a soft touch for helping kids? Is he or she the type who will respond to the plight of one child or would a global approach be better. An example of the latter is: "If this isn't funded, 20,000 children in this community will not have a summer reading program" (Somerville, personal communication, October 26, 1986). Some will only be interested in what the grant will do for their business and want only the publicity. The request must be tailored to the needs of the individual donor.

Corporations give for a wide range of reasons. Some prefer to fund only those projects that will benefit their employees, some have a real sense of social responsibility and will fund projects that will benefit the community as a whole. Knowing why a corporation gives is part of the homework that must be done before initiating a request. Getting this information includes researching the corporation and using your people skills. You must pitch a request to what the corporation is interested in. Richard Waters (1985) sums it up in this way: "We must match up the donor's needs with our needs. Hear me! I did not say match up our needs with the donor's" (p. 36).

Sometimes a donor will come to the library with a project—yes, Virginia, there is a Santa Claus. In Rhode Island, Old Stone Bank approached the state library. It wanted to fund a project that would focus on historical characters. The first year the bank gave $60,000 to fund a children's theater group that performed in branch libraries. The works performed were based on characters from historical books; and part of the funding went for the purchase of copies of the books for each branch. In the second year the grant was increased to $150,000. For the 350th anniversary of Rhode Island, the bank wanted to fund a project along the same lines as year one but using characters from Rhode Island history. There were no books available, so the bank commissioned two authors to write a book— the bank paid for its publication. The theater group will do performances based on the characters.

And how do you show appreciation for the contributions so that the next time you ask for money the donor will be favorably disposed to grant the request? When a local toy store funded one librarian's film program, she had bookmarks printed up that said: "Wayne's Toytown Cares About Kids." These were distributed at the library and at the toy store. All publicity in newspapers and the media repeated this slogan. As a follow-up and thank you for a summer reading program that was funded by two local companies, Mary Somerville prepared scrapbooks for each donor that included publicity clippings and thank you notes written by the children so that the donors would know what their contributions accomplished and with the hope that they would fund the project again next summer.

Consider cooperating with another community agency to get funding for a joint project. Some likely agencies would be boys and girls clubs, the local Y, parks and recreation departments, etc.

Do not underestimate the potential funds that can be raised from individuals. Of the total charitable dollars given by the private sector in 1984, 84 percent came from individual donors, while only 10 percent came from foundations and corporations (Klein, 1985). There are unlimited ways to raise money from individuals—limited only by your imagination. These can be a lot of fun. Some good ideas come from Barb Fierro. In Rapid City, population 40,000, $70,000 was raised in a "Pennies for Kids" campaign. Jars for pennies were placed all over the city. Student Councils pushed it, there were public service announcements, and newspaper publicity. Volunteers counted and wrapped the pennies. "Tip Me Big" was another successful fund-raiser, although on a much smaller scale. A restaurant was asked to participate. Local celebrities—e.g., senators, the mayor, etc.—served as waitpersons. People made reservations to eat and all the tips earned by the celebrities were donated to the project—amount raised, $5,000. My all-time favorite though is the "Kids for Kids" campaign which was to fund Head Start. A baby goat was delivered to a person at their place of employment. In order to get rid of the goat they had to contribute $10 to the project.

Sometimes an idea doesn't work. One that was not successful was Mary Somerville's idea to auction off an Arabian horse to help raise money for a local radio station. This didn't work because the bottom fell out of the Arabian horse market as a result of tax law changes.

The next important source of funds are state and national foundations. Applying involves more work and time because, usually, an extensive written proposal is required. Keep in mind all of the basics discussed earlier. Preparation will have a new component—i.e., researching the foundations to approach for funding. The best place to start is with the Foundation Center. The Foundation Center is a national source of information on philanthropic giving. Using its publications and its nationwide network of library reference collections, you will be able to identify foundation programs that correspond to your needs. Choose the foundations carefully. Make sure there is a match between your project and the interests of the foundation. In his book, *Grant Money and How to Get It*, Richard Boss (1980) has included an appendix which lists private foundations with a stated interest in libraries or some history of making grants to libraries (pp. 92-113). Sometimes libraries are not specifically listed as an area of interest of foundations. If this is the case, look for subjects that might cover libraries such as cultural projects or education.

The last source of contributions to mention before the presentation by Ruth Faklis's presentation on LSCA funding is of the "in-kind" variety. Falling into this category are volunteers, cooperative ventures, donations of such things as food, audiovisual materials, computers, furniture, printing and duplicating, gifts to the library, and the like. Gifts can be more trouble than they are worth. But, trust me, there can be gold in "them thar gifts." One Texas library received a gift of a collection of valuable Navajo rugs. These were prominently displayed and graciously acknowledged. The pleased donor might be a future source of contributions.

Volunteers can also be a mixed blessing. Careful selection and training of volunteers can be a substantial source of help and be worth the staff time involved in recruiting and training. The keys here are recruitment, adequate training, a show of appreciation, getting feedback, and evaluating results. Pasadena has a great system for recruiting volunteers for all government agencies. There is an office that screens the volunteers before the names are turned over to the agencies. Requests for volunteers are included in the community's electric bills. This way, every person in the community knows if, for example, the library needs volunteers. Consider tapping civic groups, senior citizens, and local businesses. And please do not overlook using teenagers as volunteers. Some companies encourage their employees to volunteer in the community and will provide release time for this purpose. One problem in the P.S. column in *Bottom Line* is "How can I figure out how much our current volunteer program costs the library" (Cassell, 1986, p. 52)? The solution is to cost out the staff time involved in writing a job description, recruiting and interviewing prospective volunteers, training, and supervision. This is useful information to have. It will determine whether enlisting volunteers is a worthwhile activity in your library.

Broaden your idea of who should serve as volunteers. The Seattle Public Library planned a showing of the film *Fame* (Van Wyk, 1985) to be followed by a panel discussion by local artists—all at no cost. The artists were delighted to contribute their time, and the program was a great success.

In small communities, particularly rural communities, there is a strong history of citizen participation and volunteerism. People are often willing to contribute their time and talents for special projects. Tailoring your need to their talent can have gratifying results. For more ideas, see the October issue of *American Libraries* (McCormick, 1986) and Irene Martin's (1984) article in *Rural Libraries*.

The best sources of tangible products are those businesses that sell the products or services you need. Try McDonalds for refreshments for the party you plan at the end of your summer reading program, or try a local photoduplicating business for having flyers printed up. The possibilities are endless.

Don't overlook cooperative ventures as a source of programming that does not involve an outlay of money, although staff time is always involved. A wonderful example is the Pasadena Arts Workshop which obtained funding to do outreach arts programs. The programming sites include the branch libraries in Pasadena, offering their children's librarian a fine opportunity to expose children to what the library has to offer in the way of arts and crafts books, puppetry, film programs, etc. And the audience consists of young people who might not already be library users, since the project targets minority and disadvantaged populations.

I have touched on a lot of issues here and all haven't been covered. There are non-LSCA grants available from government agencies such as the National Endowment for the Humanities that haven't been mentioned, but these are easy to find out about.

And as daunting as all this may seem, money does beget money, success breeds success, so be persistent and patient. Keep in mind the importance of people skills—in the final analysis, people give to people. Think of the profession of children's or young adult librarian in the broadest sense; recognize that although you probably have taken courses where you learned about book selection and book talks, planning film programs and storytelling, there is a lot more to being a children's or young adult librarian than you learned in school and that includes fundraising.

NOTES

Boss, R. W. (1980). *Grant money and how to get it: A handbook for librarians.* New York: R. R. Bowker.

Brakeley, G. A., Jr. (1980). *Tested ways to successful fund raising.* New York: AMACOM.

Cassell, K. A., ed. (1986). P.S. from our readers. *The Bottom Line: A Financial Magazine for Librarians, 1* (charter issue), 52.

Elleman, B. (1986, October). Vitalizing the school library. *Here's How, 5.*

Heyns, B. (1978). *Summer learning and the effects of schooling.* New York: Academic Press.

Klein, K. (1985). *Fundraising for social change.* Washington, DC: Center for Responsive Governance.

Margolis, B. (1986). In the news: Friends of Libraries are potent fund raisers. *The Bottom Line: A Financial Magazine for Librarians, 1* (charter issue), 7.

Martin, I. (1984). Stretching: Making a little money go.... *Rural Libraries, 4*(2), 49-53.

McCormick, E. (1986, October). Youth reach: Revitalizing the children's area. *American Libraries, 17,* 712-714.

Van Wyk, J. E. (1985, February). Seattle fame: A celebration of Seattle's young people. *Voice of Youth Advocates, 7,* 311-312.

Waters, R. (1985, Spring). Public/private relationships make it happen. *Public Library Quarterly, 6,* 27-37.

RUTH FAKLIS

Youth Services Consultant
Suburban Library System
Burr Ridge, Illinois

Part II: Funding for Youth Services— Library Services and Construction Act

When seeking funding for additional programs, special projects, expanded library services, etc., the Library Services and Construction Act (LSCA) grant monies should be considered. All fifty states are entitled to LSCA funds. Each may administer the funds a little differently; however, certain requirements are to be met by all. These include the following:

1. a state must submit a state plan of action;
2. each state must submit a five year program; and
3. each state must review and amend where necessary its approved state plan, review and revise its five year program and submit an annual program list of its projects (Corry, 1982, p. 65).

The U.S. Congress authorizes library legislation and appropriates funds for library services through the Library Services and Construction Act. These funds are allocated to the states by the U.S. Department of Education (Illinois State Library Staff, 1984, p. 4). This agency requires the state to fulfill the aforementioned obligations to obtain LSCA monies (the specific regulations for the Library Services and Construction Act may be found in volume 34 of the *Code of Federal Regulations*, chapters 74, 75, 76 and 77) (Illinois State Library Staff, 1984, p. 4).

The LSCA grant process is divided into three title programs. Each title program has specific guidelines/objectives for the grantee to adhere to when applying for funding.

Title I funds have been used to purchase library materials such as books and equipment. It may also be used for salaries, other operating expenses, for the administration of start plans, and for strengthening the capacity of state library administrative agencies to meet the needs of the people of the state (Corry, 1982, p. 66). These funds are not intended for private or special library use but rather for use by public libraries which serve *all* of the public (Corry, 1982, p. 64).

75

As a side note, it should be brought to your attention that currently the Illinois State Library is being asked by the U.S. Department of Education to return $15 million of LSCA funds which was not specifically used by "public libraries which serve all of the public." The Illinois State Library supports multitype library systems. This means that private and public, academic, high schools, and special libraries are encouraged to become full participating members of Illinois Library Systems that are multitype. Those multitype systems that have received LSCA funding for interlibrary cooperation, delivery, resource sharing, etc. have technically extended the intent of LSCA funding which again was to be used "for public libraries which serve all the public."

Although the U.S. Department of Education in no way accuses the Illinois State Library of using the funds for frivolous acts or specified misconduct, and indeed have agreed the funds were used to support effective and creative library services within the state, the fact that the LSCA funds were not directed only for use by "public libraries which serve all the public" has prompted the U.S. Department of Education to request a refund of the allocated funds. This matter is still pending and awaiting a final resolution.

A library grant submitted specifically for Title I funds must address one or more of the following seven objectives to be considered:

1. The extension of public library services to areas without such services.
2. The improvement of such services in areas where such services are inadequate.
3. Making library services more accessible to persons who, by reason of distance, residence, or physical handicap, or other disadvantage, are unable to receive the benefits of public library services regularly made available to the public.
4. Adapting public library services to meet particular needs of persons within the state, including the needs of persons in state institutions.
5. Strengthening major urban resource libraries (public libraries).
6. Improving library services to persons with limited English-speaking ability or with literacy needs.
7. Providing service through community information and referral centers (Illinois State Library Staff, 1984, p. 4).

Any public library in a system, or a system, or other library-related group may apply for a Title I grant (Illinois State Library Staff, 1984, p. 4).

Title II LSCA funds are intended for "construction of new buildings and acquisition, expansion, remodeling and alteration of existing buildings, and may be applied for by any public library or System" (Illinois State Library Staff, 1984, p. 4). Matching fund requirements for Title I and II were located via amendments to LSCA in 1977. Any federal funds expended for the administration of the LSCA act must be equally matched by state or other nonfederal funds (Corry, 1982, p. 66).

A single entity, two or more types of libraries in a system, or a system may apply for a Title III grant to plan, establish, expand, and operate cooperative networks of libraries and to plan for statewide resource sharing (Illinois State Library Staff, 1984, p. 4). Purchase of materials such as books are not fundable under the Title III grant act.

Before the actual grant proposal is written, the author must assess the needs of his/her library and community needs. Certain questions must be addressed such as how many patrons will this grant benefit, how will fulfillment of this grant improve library service to patrons, etc.? If the intent of your proposal is interagency cooperation, then cooperative planning and grant writing is necessary.

Once a determination is made on the part of the grantee as to which Title program they wish to apply to for LSCA funding, they should contact their state library or library system to ensure following the proper procedures in the application request. In most cases the information required for local funding and/or contributions would be required in the application of an LSCA grant. This includes one or more of the following concerns:
—an abstract of the project;
—a statement of philosophy or need;
—a statement of purpose for the project specifying the origins and support for its implementation;
—goals and objectives for the project including a timeline;
—procedures for the project's implementation;
—an evaluation of the project with specific regards to the goals and objectives that were sought;
—a budget which includes in-kind support;
—letter of support (Klish et al., pp. 37, 49, 75).

The author of a proposal should meet all the aforementioned components of a grant with their own writing style and delivery. This makes the proposal uniquely theirs. For the sake of the reviewer, no two grant submissions should be exactly alike in style and composition because the lack of creativity expressed may indeed be interpreted as a lack of creativity toward the proposed project. Therefore, when submitting a grant proposal, let it reflect the excitement and influence that is felt toward the fulfillment of the project.

One of the priorities in the LSCA Title I program is the programming of library service to disadvantaged persons who might not otherwise have access to such service (Corry, 1982, p. 67). In the past the term *disadvantaged* has been defined to include native Americans, blacks, foreign speaking citizens, and, more recently, senior citizens, rural farm workers, and youth (in particular, two categories of youth—preschoolers and young adults).

More and more grants are being submitted to initiate programs that will serve these "unserved." These programs will test the flexibility of the proposal for continued funding on behalf of the grantee's library in subsequent years.

Again, when seeking funding for additional programs, special projects, expanded library services, etc. the Library Services and Construction Act grant monies are available as an alternative to private and/or local sources of funding. A serious applicant should contact their state library or library system for complete grant funding information.

NOTES

Corry, E. (1982). *Grants for libraries.* Littleton, CO: Libraries Unlimited.

Illinois State Library Staff, et al. (1984). *Library Services and Construction Act grants management system operating manual.* Springfield, IL: State of Illinois.

Kalish, S. E., et al. (1983). *The proposal writer's swipe file: 15 winning fund-raising proposals...prototypes of approaches, styles and structures.* Washington, DC: Taft Corporation.

CRAIGHTON HIPPENHAMMER

Assistant Children's Services Manager
Cuyahoga County Public Library
Cleveland, Ohio

Marketing Youth Library Services:
A User Approach

Library services to youth are in crisis. New library school graduates—information managers all—are refusing to enter the field in the numbers they used to and library directors often cannot fill positions they have in youth services. School librarian positions are getting harder to fill as well. Who, after all, wants to have the sole responsibility for three or four libraries when each should be supporting a full-time professional? Young adult librarians are still looked on as optional (The Ohio Library Association just held a program called "Young Adult Service, a Right, Not a Privilege"), and children's librarians are fast becoming an endangered species in some areas of the country. Can anything be done? Does anyone care?

The answer must be a resounding yes. Library services for children are appreciated and demanded by the public. In a 1983 survey of Cuyahoga County, Ohio residents, 93 percent said library programs for children were important services for public libraries to offer second only to libraries' duty to provide information (Decision Research Corporation, 1983, pp. 34, 38). The positive impact of library summer reading programs on the reading skills of children has been demonstrated (Greene & Cummins, 1983, pp. 370-372; Heyns, 1978, p. 177), and many youth librarians experience glowing testimonies about the quality of life improvements that the library has effected in the lives of their children and young adults (Broderick, 1986, p. 118).

In the current climate of scarce tax dollars and career climbing after prestige positions, the forgetful need to be reminded and the ignorant need to be informed of the fact that youth librarians provide extremely valuable services to the community. It is time for marketing—marketing not only youth services but youth librarians themselves.

79

Definitions

What is marketing? Marketing is the series of decisions that organizations must make to effectively move their products or services to the user. Marketing is public relations with an edge. Public relations tries to influence attitudes, but marketing carefully designs programs that target specific user groups in terms of their needs and desires and programs that will bring about a change in user behavior in order to achieve organizational objectives (Kotler, 1982, p. 6).

According to Philip Kotler (1982), "[m]arketing is the philosophical alternative to force" (p. 7). Organizations try to offer their attractive marketing packages so that their powerful allure of benefits will induce a favorable response. In other words, an exchange of value is sought. The values sought from library users are expressions of tangible and intangible public support, and increased use of the services libraries provide, services that in turn satisfy user needs. It is a voluntary trade.

The User Orientation

An organization that tries to sell a product or service solely on the basis of its own personal tastes will fail. Marketing turns its attention instead on the user. Focusing on the users' needs and desires and finding ways to match them to organizational objectives will increase the use of the products and services offered.

Libraries that try to be all things to all people will end up using public monies inefficiently. If the library manager divides the library's total market into market segments—i.e., subgroups of users with similar characteristics, motivations, and desires—it will be easier to identify users' needs and wants. Then, based on the market segments identified, specific needs and services that are seldom used can be eliminated, and services that are wanted by the user can be expanded.

Most libraries also include another factor in their decision-making— i.e., the library's mission to provide quality services. Adopting a user orientation does not mean that professionals have to give up their professional expertise, but that they must communicate it better since it adds additional opinions into the equation of quality service. It is a matter of balance.

Marketing is, however, a democratic process and is antithetical to elitist approaches. The old "cultural uplift" approach of the nineteenth-century library has largely given way to providing the needs and wants of the public regardless of librarians' opinions of appropriateness (Dragon & Leisner, 1984, p. 34). The "reading ladders" model where librarians offer the next higher level of excellence in literature or the next better step in edification is not as much used in libraries today but has been replaced with meeting the expressed and perceived needs and desires of the patron. Children's librarians have much more difficulty with this trend than young adult librarians since children are less experienced, less mature, and less able to make wise decisions for themselves. Children need help and adults love to give it. Still, over the last twenty years, library service to children has moved toward giving the wants of young patrons much more attention than it used to and this is reflected in children's library collections today.

Future Trends

The process of planning new services to market in the future should involve a close look at trends in society. Visionaries such as Alvin Toffler (1970; 1980) and John Naisbitt (1982) have published valuable perspectives on current society "megatrends" and their future possibilities. The credibility of these major trends has been established in the business community and in the management literature (Conroy, 1984, p. 9). The implications for library service are strong.

There are three major trends discernible in society today that will have an increasingly strong impact on youth library services in the decades ahead. The first is that society has changed from a society based on industrial production to one based on the creation and distribution of information. New electronic information technologies are being invented so fast that it is impossible for most people to keep up with it all. Computers shrink, but their power grows. Their ability to store retrievable bits of information in ever smaller microscopic storage areas continues to progress. Although the book is not likely to be replaced soon, information is being stored in a variety of technological formats, and youth librarians must continue to be knowledgeable about them and to provide an increasing number of strategically marketed library programs involving the new technologies.

The second important trend states that as new technologies are introduced, there must be a balancing human response to ensure that the technologies are accepted. A "high touch" is needed to offset and ease the way of the "high tech." Some library programs will be aimed at making the new technology "user friendly." Other programs for youth will focus on understanding the complexities of modern life and on bringing meaning to human lives surrounded by nonhuman technologies. Continued emphasis on the youth literatures through book talks, storytelling, and reading programs will bring the greater human interaction and communication needed to cope with hard-edged technologies and an intense world.

The third important trend affecting society-at-large is that hierarchical, centralized, organizational structures are giving way to participatory, decentralized, informal networks. As individuals become more aware of choices, more willing to work for long-term considerations, and more desirous of seeking greater control over their lives, they want to participate in decisions that affect them. More and more people are preferring to exchange ideas and information as equals and hate it when someone "pulls rank." Networking methods are evolving now that connect people at all levels of organizations. The Type Z organization and the quality circle problem-solving groups are two examples. Directors and managers trained in the hierarchical model will feel increasingly frustrated if they don't change because everyone, it will seem to them, will be wanting to know all the reasons for every decision. Some administrators may feel this way already.

In the library field itself, administrators have been putting increasing importance on marketing the library. The library profession, according to *The ALA Yearbook of Library and Information Services*, "appears to be refining its attitudes away from a previous mode of bubbly, gregarious enthusiasm for PR. In its place, a more subtle, sophisticated approach to promotion has taken root. Public relations also seems to enjoy a previously unknown aura of respectability in the upper echelons of management" (Eldredge, 1986, p. 252).

Nonprofit organizations of all types have recently taken a careful, attentive approach to marketing their services and library directors have also taken to arranging their public relations efforts according to thought out plans. User-oriented marketing is not a temporary fad. In light of society "megatrends" and of trends within librarianship itself, it would seem wise for youth librarians to give the subject considerable thought— and effort as well.

Data Collection

Library services to youth reach a number of markets—e.g., preschoolers, elementary school children, young adults, parents, teachers, other professionals who work with youth, administrators, boards of trustees, community organizations, the disabled, volunteers, etc. Library markets grow and change, so identifying new groups to serve is an ongoing process.

To develop a strategy for marketing a new target group, it is necessary to collect data about them. It is helpful to know the group's needs and wants, their size, age range, location, education, lifestyle, other groups serving them, the group's likelihood of continuing with the library service under consideration, the public relations possibilities, and the cost of reaching the group. Once these factors are considered and weighed against library resources, it is possible to determine whether an effective change or addition to services can be made.

Once the target group is using library services, more information needs to be collected to determine patterns of use. Analyzed data can lead to tailoring the service even closer to the needs of the user. The recent interest in output measures by library administrators underscores their interest in gathering information about users and reinforces the recognition of library directors' increased user orientation. Youth librarians should also use output data as it can provide additional information in designing programs and in managing their collections (Hippenhammer, 1986, pp. 309-13).

The Marketing Mix

Most people think of marketing in terms of selling and advertising. This is not surprising since it is estimated that the average consumer is bombarded with 1600 messages of advertisement throughout the course of one day (Fox, 1984, p. 328). But marketing is much more than selling. It offers several techniques that managers can use to cover the broad spectrum of factors that influence buying (using) behavior. These techniques are called product, price, distribution, and promotion. Blending these tools to produce an effective marketing package is called designing the marketing mix (Kotler, 1982, p. 8).

The first technique involves examining five controllable characteristics of the product: styling, features, quality, packaging, and branding (Kotler, 1982, pp. 292-95). The distinctive look or "feel" of a product is its "styling." A warm, brightly-colored children's room will attract users more than a cold imposing one, for example. Optional product components that can be changed without altering its essence are called "features." Adding a celebrity visit to one's summer reading club may be optional, but it may help in getting free media publicity. The "quality" of a service is its perceived level of performance over time and "packaging" is the larger situation or surroundings that contain the service. Library architecture, children's room arrangement, and shelving design are all examples of packaging. Lastly, giving brand names or logos to products is an attempt to identify and distinguish them as different from the competition's products, usually as more unique or prestigious. Renaming libraries "media centers" is an example of this "branding."

The second technique of marketing is pricing. The problem with encouraging the marketing of libraries is that demands may outstrip resources. In the profit sector, price acts as a control on demand but in nonprofit libraries demand is usually limited through library policies (e.g., restrictions on telephone reference questions and on the number of videotapes circulated) and staff behavior (from shushing to policing youth behavior). Generally, libraries try to provide "free" service to maximize use, but every service has its costs, whether it is invisible tax support, a trade-off in other services not provided, or inconvenience.

The third marketing technique is distribution. Libraries must make their services available and accessible to their potential users. The design, location, and number of facilities will affect library use. Other common ways to distribute library services have been to use bookmobiles, make classroom visits, or deliver kits of library materials to outreach centers.

The last marketing technique is promotion. Publicity is the most widely used type of promotion in libraries. Publicity is the nonpaid, favorable attention given to a product or service through various media and published as significant news (Kotler, 1982, p. 355). Youth librarians are strong on producing flyers, posters, bulletin boards, press releases, newsletters, and bibliographies, but not so strong on making television and radio appearances, giving speeches, or creating news events. In-person selling (i.e., building goodwill) and paid advertising are other forms of promotion that work and that should also be examined for use in different library settings.

Gaining Credibility

The bulk of public relations is doing the job well and reminding others of that quality. On regularly scheduled occasions, however, librarians should plan and execute the new and or unusual service or marketing project. Perhaps a dusty, old, not-much-used service needs a new polishing or a library image of one kind or another needs updating. For example: Little Miss Muffet / Sat on a tuffet / Eating her curds and whey. / Along came a spider / And sat down beside her / And frightened Miss Muffet away.

Miss Muffet, in this age of feminism, has an image problem. Few self-respecting librarians of either sex today would ever admit publicly to being frightened by something as insignificant as a spider. But one must ask what technological spiders are sitting down beside youth librarians these days and what are their reactions? No doubt, a second verse for poor little Miss Muffet is needed. Big Bad Giant / Sat on his Reliant / Eating his Big Mac with cheese. / He whistled at Ms. Muffett / Who told him to stuff it / And kicked him one right on the knees.

Gaining credibility for youth library services is a difficult business. Libraries in society are generally invisible—e.g., libraries were not even mentioned in *A Nation at Risk* (National Commission on Excellence in Education, 1983)—and within the library profession, service to children is generally invisible and neglected (White, 1983, pp. 97-99).

Countering the invisibility of youth library services must be approached by confronting several market segments. The first market to address is the library administrator or principal. Youth librarians need to be seen as managers or as part of the managerial team in order to carry some weight in decision-making. Unfortunately, being creative and offering creative programs is often seen as incompatible with being an effective manager. It is perhaps understandable that administrators feel this way if they regularly see children's librarians in clown suits.

There are, however, several ways to gain credibility with administrators: (1) provide a solid program of substance and save the flash for key public relations moments; (2) regularly communicate that substance to the administrator through monthly and special reports as well as in person; (3) be cooperative in projects the administrator wants tried; and (4) never let the administrator or other professionals get away with accusing a youth librarian of having fun on the job. After all, it is work and hard work at that. If you are having fun, keep it under your hat.

Parents, teachers, and other professionals who serve youth are important additional markets with whom youth librarians should build strong relationships. Do this by communicating—even marketing—one's services to them, by cooperating in projects with them, and by treating their children right. Treating young library patrons with the same courtesy and consideration adults would get will not only impress them but their parents and teachers as well.

The most important markets to confront are the children and young adults themselves. Get to know their wants and needs and then provide library materials and services to meet them. Student advisory councils have worked well, especially with young adults. Ask for their opinions. Spend a small part of the materials budget on their fads and hot topics and enter into and be able to discuss their current interests. Several "with-it" posters in the library can do wonders for public relations and make the library a more comfortable place to visit. Keeping the library alive and sensitive to its many varied markets and meeting patrons well are two precepts that account for 90 percent of effective library service (Hunsicker, 1973, p. 120). Adequately communicating that good performance to the public so it is publicly appreciated is effective public relations. Credibility is based on just such recognized, consistent, competent performance.

Acting Now for the Future

Having looked at some major trends in society and at the need for a marketing user orientation, what specific actions can be taken to improve the public relations of, and the future of, library service to youth? There are three areas where improvements can be made. The first is to identify new market segments (new publics). One such market segment is preschoolers in day-care centers and day-care homes. Preschoolers in day-care homes and their caregivers are a group virtually untouched by targeted library service and the need is great. During 1985, 39 percent of all three-and-four-year-olds were enrolled in preschool compared to 11 percent twenty years earlier, and between 75 and 90 percent of all family day-care facilities are unlicensed or unregistered (Brophy, 1986, p. 60).

A second market segment is latchkey school-age children. This group is a growing societal phenomenon and cooperative programs with other community agencies are needed.

A third market segment involves youth in crisis. Library information and referral programs for youth with drug problems, suicide intentions, need for abortion alternatives, etc. or cooperation with community programs, hot-lines and other in-place civic organization aids should continue to be established.

The last two potential markets, home schools and the new conservative parochial schools, have grown remarkably in the last decade with the rise of the new conservatism, and both have little or no library service. Careful communication will be the key to serving these two groups successfully.

The second area where improvements should meet the future of library service to youth is in polishing the image of the youth librarian.

1. The concept of generic librarians, known by some as generalists, must be fought. This model of library service has been devastating to the age subject specialties and to service to youth. Children and young adults need librarians deeply knowledgeable in their literatures.
2. Youth librarians must be seen as *public* service professionals. Making a children's librarian catalog juvenile books in a back corner is wasting a public service talent and wasting public relations opportunities. Hiring a young adult librarian who likes to catalog books is like hiring a reference librarian who hates to answer the phone.
3. Publicize awards and recognitions won by youth librarians.
4. Highlight successful youth librarians in both local and national media.
5. Train speakers to promote not only the youth literatures but also the youth library business. All youth librarians should be trained to see themselves as PR ambassadors but a handful of especially fluent and verbal "personalities" should be subsidized to argue and enhance the case at the national level, both within and without the profession. The youth associations within ALA could gather the research studies, anecdotes, and other supportive material in a handy form for background information for persuasive speech making.
6. Youth librarians should mentor and recruit public service talent into their fields.
7. Start establishing a corporate image for "youth library services" by developing the recognizable, visual identity of a logo or symbol. Done

right, branding can be a powerful public relations tool.

The third area where changes should be made is in fine-tuning library services to the trends of the future and to their public relations impact:

1. Include patron use data in managing youth library collections, particularly in additional copy acquisition and weeding decisions.
2. Budget for special public relations programs.
3. Examine opportunities within the community for outreach, particularly within the political arena—e.g., Cuyahoga County Public Library's 1986 Summer Reading Club theme was "Hooray for the U.S.A.!" a theme that tied in nicely with the Statue of Liberty centennial celebrations, and one that gave many local politicians the opportunity to participate in patriotic celebrations at their local library. The governor of Ohio also awarded a citation of merit and letters of congratulations to reading club participants.
4. Delegate preschool story hours to well-trained assistants so the professional can concentrate on the more difficult toddler and school-age story hours.
5. Increase the use of puppets and puppet shows to extend children's literature to wider audiences.
6. Encourage the telling of literary stories in a nonmemorized, storytelling style.
7. Look for ways to mesh new technologies with current library practice—e.g., create a literary pen pal book reviewing club using electronic bulletin boards and modems to encourage young readers to recommend books to their peers.
8. Start a juvenile videotape collection that circulates to children.

Conclusion

As the twenty-first century approaches, it is imperative that youth librarians look to identifying new library user groups and tailoring services to their needs. Areas of service most likely to grow will be: (1) technological forms of information (high tech); (2) human responses through literature and nurturing (high touch); and (3) democratic and egalitarian approaches to supplying user wants and needs (direct touch). The techniques of marketing are ideally suited to addressing these needs of the future.

Needs assessment is an ongoing process that demands constant reevaluation. After data collection from market segment users, it may be found that Miss Muffet's new image as updated earlier is too sharp and a modified image is needed: Little Ms. Muffet / Can rough it and tough it / And face up to problems galore. / Demanding and gaining / Assertiveness training, / She flinches at spiders no more.

The world needs to be told that youth librarians are a new breed. The assertive, knowledgeable, creative talent in the youth library field is impressive. Yes, youth services must be marketed, but the profession needs to market its most valuable resource—its own personnel—the professional youth librarian.

NOTES

Broderick, D. M., (Ed.) (1986, August/October). Guest editorial. *Voice of Youth Advocates, 9*, 118.

Brophy, B. (1986, 27 October). Children under stress. *U.S. News and World Report, 101*, 60.

Conroy, B. (1984). Megatrend marketing: Creating the library's future. In G. T. Ford (Ed.), *Marketing and the library* (pp. 9-17). New York: Haworth Press.

Decision Research Corporation. (1983). *A survey of attitudes towards the Cuyahoga County Public Library*. Cleveland: DRC.

Dragon, A. C., & Leisner, T. (1984). The ABCs of implementing library marketing. In G. T. Ford (Ed.), *Marketing and the library* (pp. 34-41). New York: Haworth Press.

Eldredge, J. (1986). Public relations. In R. Parent (Ed.), *ALA yearbook of library and information services: A review of library events 1985*. (Vol. 11) (pp. 252-53). Chicago: ALA.

Fox, S. R. (1984). *The mirror makers: A history of American advertising and its creators*. New York: Morrow.

Greene, E., & Cummins, J. (1983, Summer). Reading, libraries, and summer achievement. *Top of the News, 39*, 370-372.

Heyns, B. (1978). *Summer learning and the effects of schooling*. New York: Academic Press.

Hippenhammer, C. (1986, Spring). Managing children's library collections through objective data. *Top of the News, 42*, 309-313.

Hunsicker, Marya. (1973). Public relations in a children's room. In A. Angoff (Ed.), *Public relations for libraries: Essays in communications techniques* (pp. 117-31). Westport, CT: Greenwood Press.

Kotler, P. (1982). *Marketing for nonprofit organizations* (2nd ed). Englewood Cliffs, NJ: Prentice-Hall.

Matthews, A. J. (1984). Library market segmentation: An effective approach for meeting client needs. In G. T. Ford (Ed.), *Marketing and the library* (pp. 20-26). New York: Haworth Press.

Naisbitt, J. (1982). *Megatrends: Ten new directions transforming our lives*. New York: Warner Books.

The National Commission on Excellence in Education. (1983). *A nation at risk: The imperative for educational reform*. Washington, DC: The Commission.

O'Brien, P. M. (1981, Spring). An administrator speaks of services to youth. *Top of the News, 37*, 243-246.

Toffler, A. (1980). *Third wave*. New York: Morrow.

Toffler, A. (1970). *Future shock*. New York: Random House.

White, L. J. (1983). *The public library in the 1980s: The problems of choice*. Lexington, MA: Lexington Books.

MARGARET BUSH
Assistant Professor
Graduate School of Library & Information Science
Simmons College
Boston, Massachusetts

The Right Stuff: Recruitment and Education for Children's and Young Adult Specialists

"There was something ancient, primordial, irresistible about the challenge of this stuff, no matter what a sophisticated and rational age one might think he lived in" (Wolfe, 1984, p. 22). In his exploration of the bonds of fraternity among the military test pilots who achieved heroic status as the early astronauts, Tom Wolfe was fascinated by an almost tangible but undefinable central quality by which its members were ranked. Energy, guts, bravery, idealism, and more seemed obvious traits, but somewhere beyond these lay an "ineffable quality" implicitly understood by the men in this special brotherhood. Theirs was a time of striving for recognition, for pride, and for legitimacy as they tested and extended the limits of their specialized occupation. In time they gained not only glory, but, more importantly, acceptance by their peers. And then the institutional structure in which they worked and the very world itself changed. Having achieved their place as "deserving occupants at the top of the pyramid of the right stuff" (Wolfe, 1984, p. 366), the importance of the fraternity and the ideal began to slip away.

Not long ago a friend and colleague who is the head of children's services in a public library serving a community of about 40,000 was reflecting on problems of assessing the background and skills of applicants for a position as children's librarian. She was pointing out that the academic and work experiences listed on the résumé and application are often not very reliable indicators of the actual education or training the individual has been provided. "You simply can't assume any common set of competencies," she commented. While the common sense of this seems pretty basic, don't we usually suppose that if a person has taken the requisite courses in library school, there will be at least a passing acquaintance with some widely understood tenets of children's literature, say, or school librarianship or young adult services?

A similar but more formal set of statements regarding competencies was developed by Patsy Perritt and Kathleen Heim in an article for the Winter 1987 issue of *Top of the News* on the ALA-accredited master's degree as the basic professional credential for youth services librarians. They observe that: "National standards for youth services in librarianship, except for those in the school setting, have not been developed, utilized, and promoted by members of the profession, and this is one of the reasons educational programs for youth services lack centrality" (Perritt & Heim, 1987, p. 154). One might add that, on an informal level, we do have something of a centrality of belief about the personal and professional characteristics and skills desirable for youth services librarians. We have pretty commonly held ideas about the right stuff for librarians serving children and adolescents, and these tend to be both rooted in long abiding ideals and to have developed some new tenets in response to shifts in management theory and political realities in libraries and schools. We have a strong collegiality based on idealism, pragmatism, and frustration about our status in the larger library profession. It is true that we have not developed structured definitions and programs which might effectively put youth services at the height we believe it deserves on the pyramid of librarianship.

What then is the right stuff? Who has the responsibility for identifying and developing it? How well is this being done? What can we as library educators, youth services librarians, and members of professional organizations do to make sure that it is done better? The following discussion will look at some of the formulations of professional competencies, comment on the relationship of these to curriculum offerings in library schools, examine some current issues and problems in professional education for youth services specialists, and finally suggest some action items for the agenda we hope will emerge from this Allerton conference.

Professional Qualifications

What about the contention that we don't have a set of national youth services standards upon which to construct and evaluate professional education? In the strictest sense this is true, of course, but let us look at the content and similarities in existing documents. The school library/media field, being both the most complex and the most formulated, is the logical place to begin. The national standards published in 1975 and to be replaced in the near future, stipulate that: "The media specialist holds a master's degree in media from a program that combines library and information science, educational communications and technology, and curriculum." This academic program is to develop a specified list of competencies, including, among others, planning and administration, analysis of user characteristics and information needs, media design and production, and interpretation and application of research (American Association of School Librarians, 1975, pp. 22-23).

It is not mandated that the master's degree be from an accredited library school, and, as has been widely noted and discussed, school media specialists are subject to the requirements of certification regulations set by the individual states. From a pragmatic point of view, state regulations, being a condition of employment, generally take precedence over the national standards which lack a structured means of enforcement. Sometimes the national and state requirements are similar or even congruent. As noted in Ann Franklin's 1984 survey of school library media certification requirements in each state, published in the January 1984 *School Library Journal*, some states include a requirement of an MLS, some levels of certification require a master's degree plus additional hours of study, and in many cases a number of stipulated hours short of a master's degree will suffice (Franklin, 1984, pp. 21-34). Presumably the lack of uniform application of the national standard causes some difficulty for individuals wishing to relocate from one state to another.

Not only do the academic requirements and desired competencies for school library media specialists differ widely among states, but there are distinctly different opinions in the library education field as to whether the accredited library schools are the most appropriate providers of professional education for such specialists. Jane Hannigan, in a wide-ranging examination of library education, has advocated moving "all educational responsibility for this professional to schools of education" (Hannigan, 1984, p. 55). Perritt and Heim (1987), anxious to further the commonalities among youth services in the library schools and in professional practice, admit that one of the most important of the unresolved problems is "professional consensus as to the location of the educational component" (p. 156). In this largest of the youth specialties, and the only one to actually have national standards, there is no centrality as described earlier by these authors.

While there are no functional national standards for children's and young adult services, the widely recognized "Competencies for Librarians Serving Youth," developed by ALA's Young Adult Services Division (YASD), is generally considered prescriptive and useful as a guide for professional education and for the development of library positions. This document does not specify a level of academic achievement but stipulates specific areas of knowledge and skills pertaining to: leadership and professionalism, knowledge of the client group, communication, administration, knowledge of materials, access to information, and services. Competencies involved in knowledge of the client group include applying factual and interpretive information on adolescent psychology, growth and development, sociology, and popular culture and also knowledge of the reading process in planning for materials and services. The management skills include identification and development of external funding, applying and conducting research, and monitoring legislation. Service capabilities include two that have been particular philosophical tenets of the young adult services field—i.e., crisis intervention counseling and involving young adults in planning and implementing services for their age group (Young Adult Services Division, 1982, p. 51). The Board of Directors of the Association for Library Service to Children (ALSC) (1986) recently adopted recommendations of a long-range planning task force which included the development of a set of competencies for children's librarians, and the task has been assigned to the division's education committee.

In the absence of national children's services standards, many state library agencies and professional associations have developed standards in recent years or are now in the process of doing so. The *Standards for Youth Services in Public Libraries of New York State* include a list of competencies which are a close adaptation of the YASD competencies. Since the title of the original document designates "youth" rather than "young adults," the New York task force simply substituted the same term throughout the document wherever "young adults" had been used to designate the client group with a resulting list intended for use with both children's and young adult librarians. No indication is given of competencies which might be more germane to either one of the services. The YASD list was apparently intended primarily for use in library education since the competencies were all designated for "the student"; the New York list assigns them for "the librarian" (New York Library Association, 1984).

The competencies stated in the standards for school library media centers are not markedly different from the YASD competencies, and, although both are probably due for further examination and discussion, there does seem to be enough common ground to develop a central set of skills and characteristics for librarians serving youth, both children and adolescents, whether in a public library setting or a school library media center.

Competencies which are agreed upon and promulgated by national organizations set one sort of standard for professional education. Another useful standard is level of academic achievement. The master's degree from an ALA accredited library school has been the generally accepted requirement for entry into professional librarianship, but, as previously mentioned, different requirements often apply to a very substantial segment of the field, namely school librarianship. What of children's and young adult services in public libraries? Several of the state level standards recommend (most do not require) an M.L.S. for the librarian responsible for youth services at the local library. A number of state surveys of children's services provide interesting information about the academic credentials actually held by children's librarians. A 1978 survey of Illinois public libraries, for example, focused on many aspects of thirty-two libraries selected, among other reasons, for their reputed strength in services to children. It was found that seventeen, or a little better than 50 percent, of the librarians had an M.L.S. Six librarians had bachelor's degrees, and eight (25 percent) had less than a bachelor's degree (Richardson, 1978, pp. 136-137). A more recently published survey of 285 children's librarians in Michigan revealed that 136 (47.7 percent) had an M.L.S. In this instance, sixty-six individuals (23.1 percent) had less than a bachelor's degree, while the remaining eighty-three had bachelor's degrees or other degrees and certificates. In this study, 7.7 percent of the librarians were noted as attending school, but the levels of study were not specified. It was also found that 67 percent of the respondents had earned continuing education units (CEUs) (Todara, et al., 1985, p. 5).

The information from these surveys are important parts of the demographics of our profession—a subject to be explored further in this program—which raise questions about professional competencies and credentials for youth services librarians. Provided we accept the assumption that the M.L.S. is desirable as the entry-level professional requirement, how can we encourage its achievement by more librarians? Is it reasonable to suppose that all public and school libraries could or should have professionally educated librarians? How do we define professional? What are the educational needs and requirements of those youth services librarians who have not earned the professional degree? Clearly, various states have been struggling with some of these questions, though we lack cohesive information about the results of state efforts which we might draw upon for a strong national system on which to plan and promote professional education in youth services.

Just as all states have certification requirements, some states also certify librarians for the public library field—usually on the basis of less complex requirements. The subject of certification is by no means new, but in recent years some writers have suggested that this idea deserves attention in the national scheme of regulating professional credentials. Standards and a mechanism for certification are sometimes advocated—and disputed—as an alternative to the present scheme of the M.L.S. as the preferred basic requirement (see Willett, 1984, pp. 13-23). Certification may also be seen as a system for ensuring competency at various levels of professional responsibility, and this notion ought to be considered at a national level as a potential means of strengthening both the provision of library services to youth and the role of youth services librarianship in the larger professional field.

Aside from philosophical interests and concern about professionalism, there is a very practical matter which lends urgency to the notions of competencies and certification. At the present time the demand for librarians in the youth services specialties outstrips by far the supply of candidates entering the field through library schools. John Berry (1986) strongly stated the shortage of children's and young adult librarians in a recent *Library Journal* editorial (p. 4). The accompanying report on national placements of library school graduates for 1985 showed more librarians placed in public libraries than in any other type—a situation occurring for the first time since 1977. Moreover, of the 2,387 placements, 313 (13 percent) were in youth services with an almost even split between public and school librarians. The three largest specialties were children's services in public libraries (113 positions), children's services in school libraries (112 positions), and business libraries (100 positions). Additionally, there were forty-five placements in youth services in public libraries, forty in youth services in school libraries, and three in children's services "other" (Learmont & Van Houten, 1986, p. 35). It must be admitted that some large areas of librarianship, such as reference services, were not delineated in the specialty listings, but youth services librarians are nonetheless an impressive population among the recently placed graduates of library schools.

Placements of graduates are only one part of the supply and demand picture. We don't have an accurate accounting of the total number of professional vacancies nationwide, but, based on records for just one region, one can surmise that there is a very large shortfall. In New England alone there were 771 professional positions posted during 1985. The library school at Simmons—with by far the largest number of placements of any library school—placed only 141 graduates (Learmont & Van Houten, pp. 32-33). Thirteen of the graduates were placed in foreign countries and another 11 went to states outside the region, leaving 123 individuals to fill only about 16 percent of the vacancies. Youth services positions numbered 159 (20.6 percent) of the total (Simmons College, 1986). Much smaller numbers of placements were made by the library schools at Southern Connecticut University and the University of Rhode Island, and presumably a few individuals came into the region from other states. However, the gap is still large, and faculty and administration at Simmons would testify from the numbers of phone calls from desperate library administrators that the crisis is of far greater proportions than indicated in the *Library Journal* survey.

The shortage of library school graduates has several implications for youth services. Some vacant positions—even those offering fine salaries—are going unfilled. Some are being filled by graduates who did not anticipate going into these specialties and had no relevant specialty coursework at all. Some are being filled by so-called preprofessionals, who have widely divergent amounts and kinds of experience. Some of them will settle in comfortably and perform very competently while others will struggle along at a mediocre level; all can be paid lower salaries than a professional candidate.

The Massachusetts Library Association is busily developing children's services standards which will state competencies and recommend an M.L.S. children's librarian for every library (Massachusetts Library Association, 1988). A large part of the impetus for developing standards in this instance came from library administrators concerned about the current shortage of qualified children's librarians. State certification of children's librarians has been discussed but only tentatively. This is a state and a region that has employed effective recruitment strategies for youth services—e.g., excellent coverage of the shortage in metropolitan and suburban newspapers, a slide-tape presentation to encourage library trustees to support professional levels of children's services, and a brochure on youth services careers for distribution by local libraries to high schools and colleges. Children's librarians have worked with their professional colleagues to pass minimum salary recommendations for the state; while salaries are certainly uneven in the state, there has been a noticeable upward trend since the minimum salary has been advocated (and the level has been raised three times in just a few years). Enrollment in the youth services courses at Simmons is strong and rising but still falls far short of the demand since many of these students already fill professional positions. The complexities of recruitment have received attention in national programs and journals, but the national professional organizations have not moved beyond discussion to a strong, concerted program or projects to address the problem.

Librarians sometimes tend to blame the library schools for failures both in attracting students to the field and in educating them adequately to meet library needs. The general antipathy between practicing professionals and library schools has been variously documented (Conant, 1980) and has certainly been shared in part by youth services librarians. The widespread assumption that library schools don't support youth services was exacerbated in the early 1980s when library schools in several states were closing, declining to fill faculty positions in the youth services specialties, or transferring responsibility for the youth services curriculum to other schools or departments of the parent institution. State professional associations did battle with the library schools in several instances, and the youth divisions of ALA endorsed their efforts and expressed concern to library school deans. Some efforts succeeded in gaining renewed support of youth services in the library schools, but others failed, leaving great gaps in professional education in some parts of the country.

One study was undertaken by this author and Melody Allen, consultant for children's services at the Rhode Island State Library, to document the alleged deterioration of support for youth services in the library schools. A survey of all the accredited schools was conducted in the spring of 1985 asking about course offerings, faculty, enrollment, continuing education, and other matters. The results were encouraging in many respects but did not provide the desired comprehensive view since just thirty-eight of the sixty-seven schools (56.7 percent) accredited at the time provided usable returns. There was evidence of a good array of regularly offered core courses in children's and young adult services and school librarianship in the majority of schools. Courses tended to be offered by tenured or tenure-track faculty, and the number of these positions was healthy if not large—a fact that seems even more positive when viewed in light of the published placement figures for the individual schools (Allen & Bush, 1987). These would suggest quite small enrollments in youth services specialties in many cases; it was notable that schools often did not provide enrollment information. It was not possible to establish enrollment trends for the three-year period queried. The returns indicated very few students doing advanced level specialization beyond the M.L.S.—a very serious situation in a set of specialties badly in need of deepening and strengthening their theoretical base. The most positive information gleaned in the study was the array of faculty interests, projects, and teaching responsibilities. Several schools known to have strong youth services faculty did not respond to the survey, and, even without these individuals, the pool of talent and leadership reflected in the returns was truly impressive.

The leadership of library school faculty in the youth services fields merits attention since these individuals have been particularly effective in professional associations in recent years. In ALA's Association for Library Service to Children (ALSC), three of the past five presidents were library educators, and, during several of these years, faculty have also served as presidents of the American Association of School Librarians (AASL) and of the Young Adult Services Division (YASD). Many more such individuals have served on the divisions' boards of directors and have chaired committees; some have gone on to major responsibilities in other units of ALA. These individuals continue to provide leadership, to keep our interests very much alive in the library schools, and to contribute significantly to development of professional programs such as this Allerton conference. (The notion of a national conference of children's, school, and young adult librarians to forge a joint agenda for the future was first proposed by Shirley Aaron of Florida State University when she was president of AASL and was further developed by a very active ALSC and YASD member, Leslie Edmonds of the University of Illinois.) Though bonds between a significant number of library educators and other youth services professionals are indeed strong, it probably cannot be said that librarians in these specialties have any greater trust of library schools than their other librarian colleagues. It may well be, however, that we don't actually suffer the practitioner/educator gap to the degree sometimes noted in parts of the library field. In looking toward a future agenda, there ought to be opportunity for further creative partnerships and collaborations.

In spite of the noted commitment of many library schools to youth services, we still don't have adequate information about the actual quality of professional education in these specialties, and, of course, it is known informally that there is a lack of good course offerings at some schools. As library schools have suffered declining enrollments and some have been closed in recent years, a growing number of writers have suggested that the professional schools ought to become individually more specialized rather than each trying to serve the broad spectrum of librarianship. Ralph Conant, in his well-known study of library education sponsored by ALA and funded by the H. W. Wilson Co., strongly recommended a national plan which would further decrease the number of schools and would "recommend an appropriate distribution of specializations among the surviving library schools" (Conant, 1980, p. 62). Jane Anne Hannigan, long-time library educator and youth services specialist, also raised this possibility in a substantial examination of how excellence might be achieved in library education. "[P]erhaps the time has come for library schools to recognize that they can be qualitatively superior only by limiting the number of specialized programs they offer and thus concentrating limited resources" (Hannigan, 1984, p. 6).

Such suggestions of narrowing the focus of schools and decreasing the specializations of each school are more than a little unsettling to youth services librarians since they suspect that library schools would follow the example of many public libraries and school districts that have cut back support for library services to children and adolescents in bad financial times. This might not be exactly the case since library schools do respond (at least somewhat) to the demands of the marketplace, and there are increased postings and placements in youth services.

The shortage of librarians is widespread, occurring in many parts of the country, and of course many individuals who are potential youth services librarians are women with families who are returning to the work force—most would be unable to go to another state for their professional education. We must continue to provide a basic level of specialization in youth services in every library school. But we must also look more carefully at the proposition of identifying, promoting, and building upon those programs which offer greater depth of specialization. In a recent article on the future of services to young adults, Gerald Hodges (1987), a faculty member at the University of Iowa and long active in the leadership of YASD, proposes that the three ALA youth divisions make it a top priority to identify several programs and develop funding to support these as models or centers of strong specialization (p. 173).

While the earlier discussion focuses on library schools, these institutions are by no means the sole providers of youth services professional education. Continuing education, in-service training, and self-development are all essential in building the skills and knowledge of youth services librarians. As with the academic programs, there is a lack of comprehensive information and consensus about what needs to be provided and how best to provide it. In some cases there is cooperation between libraries, professional associations, and library schools to plan and provide educational opportunities, but, generally, communication and shared planning are haphazard. This is not to suggest that all education has to be jointly sponsored or conform to some master plan, but it seems obvious that educational opportunity for the individual youth services librarian could be strengthened considerably through the clarifying of roles and increased sharing of assessment and planning. The reporting of good programs is not always as full or widespread as we might like, but, as with the academic offerings, there are very good models upon which to build. A recent example is an Iowa program reported in considerable detail in the *Rural Library Service Newsletter* (Cresap, 1986, p. 14). Planned by Marilyn Nickelsberg of the State Library of Iowa for children's librarians and public library directors responsible for children's services in rural communities, this program was intended to provide management training for staff who have little or no professional education. The intensive two-day program gave some seventy-five librarians an opportunity to acquire new insights and techniques for planning, developing, and assessing children's services. In addition to informative content and a stimulating format, this program was exemplary in other ways. The planner was extremely effective in collaborating—she selected a children's consultant from another state library and a faculty member from a distant library school as her presenters and had them share the program planning from the outset. She also publicized and documented the program carefully, fully intending that other states be encouraged to emulate this effort. Her well-attended, substantial program served both her audience and other education providers very well indeed.

There is a great mass of workshops, programs, and training sessions which provide educational opportunities to youth services librarians each year at the local, state, national, and even international level. Some of these respond to local needs and others to very specialized interests, while others have widespread appeal and may or may not be well publicized. In this so-called information age, it would be wonderful indeed if we had some central mechanism for collecting and disseminating information about educational program offerings; theoretically, at least, this would provide greater opportunity for individuals to avail themselves of programs and would also enable us to discern the patterns of what is being provided and what might be missing.

There are many issues related to nonacademic educational opportunities which need to be addressed. The previously mentioned survey of library schools included a component on continuing education offerings which indicated programs in a broad range of subject areas. However, the most frequently offered programs and those with the highest attendance were predominantly those concerned with children's books and storytelling. Programs related to computers were also offered somewhat frequently, and there were fewer offerings related to management of youth services (Allen & Bush, 1987). Lacking a strong philosophical and theoretical basis in regard to education and training, program providers generally respond to the marketplace, offering what they believe the clientele wants and/or needs. Needs assessment as part of program planning, motivating youth services staff toward more diverse professional development, and better funding for educational opportunities are all subjects which ought to be on our agenda.

Youth services have been largely driven by idealism and energy. In recent years, with shifting economic, social, and political winds and changes in institutional structures and practices, we've begun to find legitimacy and status in the larger realm of librarianship being tested. The questions of defining, developing, and demonstrating individual competencies are critical. The tasks are challenging, and the climate is excellent for accomplishing them—the current shortage of youth services librarians has created a wide awareness of our value, and our leadership is more widely respected at all levels than we have realized. We must seize the moment and develop an agenda to:

1. Enlarge and strengthen recruitment efforts.
2. Clarify our definition of essential competencies and establish desired levels of competence.
3. Deal with the complex issues of professional credentials and certification.
4. Strengthen youth librarians' theoretical base and support advanced specialization.
5. Develop better communication, coordination, and planning between various categories of education providers.
6. Develop and support model programs in library schools, libraries, and professional associations.

NOTES

Allen, M. L., & Bush, M. (1987, Winter). Library education and youth services: A survey of faculty, course offerings and related activities in accredited library schools. *Library Trends, 35*, 485-508.

American Association of School Librarians. (1975). *Media programs, district and school.* Chicago: American Library Association; and Washington, DC: Association for Educational Communications and Technology.

Association for Library Services to Children, American Library Association. (1986). *Minutes, ALSC board of directors meetings.* ALA Annual Conference.

Berry J. (1986, October 15). The next shortage of librarians. *Library Journal, 111*, 4.

Conant, R. W. (1980). *The Conant report, a study of the education of librarians.* Cambridge, MA: The MIT Press.

Cresap, M. (1986, August). Kids are rural, too! *Rural Library Service Newsletter, 6*, 1-4.

Franklin, A. Y. (1984, January). School library media certification requirements: 1984 update. *School Library Journal, 30*, 21-34.

Hannigan, J. A. (1984). *Vision to purpose to power: A quest for excellence in the education of library and information science professionals.* Washington, DC: Office of Educational Research and Improvement, Center for Libraries and Education Improvement.

Hodges, G. G. (1987, Winter). The future of youth services: Developmental, demographic, and educational concerns. *Top of the News, 43*, 167-175.

Learmont, C., & Van Houten, S. (1986, October 15). Placements and salaries 1985: Little change. *Library Journal, 111*, 31-38.

Massachusetts Library Association. (1986). *Children's services standards.* Draft, October. [Boston?]: MLA.

New York Library Association, Youth Services Section, Task Force on Standards for Youth Services. (1984). *Standards for youth services in public libraries of New York State.* New York: NYLA.

Richardson, S. K. (1978). *An analytical survey of Illinois public library service to children.* Springfield, IL: Illinois State Library.

Perritt, P. H., & Heim, K. M. (1987, Winter). ALA-accredited master's degree: Considerations for youth services librarianship. *Top of the News, 43*, 149-155.

Simmons College, Graduate School of Library and Information Science. (1986). Placement statistics for graduates, 1985. New England job vacancies by specialization.

Todaro, J. B., et al. (1985). *Children's services in public libraries: Research and assessment for Michigan.* Lansing, MI: Michigan Library Association.

Willett, H. G. (1984, Summer). Certification and education for library and information science. *Journal of Education for Library and Information Science, 25*, 13-23.

Wolfe, T. (1984). *The right stuff.* New York: Bantam.

Young Adult Services Division, American Library Association. (1982, September). Young adults deserve the best: Competencies for librarians serving youth. *School Library Journal, 29*, 51.

ADDITIONAL NOTES

Atkinson, J. L. (1983). Library education for young adult specialists. In E. V. LiBretto (Ed.), *New directions for young adult services* (pp. 163-79). New York: R. R. Bowker.

Egan, B. (1981, May/June). The role of the children's librarian as a professional librarian: A position paper. *Emergency Librarian, 8*(5), 13-16.

Fitzgibbons, S. (1983, Fall). Children's librarianship: The unmet personnel needs. *New Jersey Libraries, 16*, 8-17.

Fitzgibbons, S. (1982, May/June). Research on library services for children and young adults: Implications for practice. *Emergency Librarian, 9*(5), 6-17.

Greer, R. C. (1980). Information transfer: A conceptual model for librarianship, information science and information management with implications for library education. In *Communicating information* (Proceedings of the American Society for Information Science conference, Anaheim, CA, 1980) (Vol. 17, pp. 373-75). New York: Knowledge Industry Publications.

Kinnell, M. (1986, Spring). Changing childhood?: A state of the art review. *International Review of Children's Literature and Librarianship, 1*(1), 33-41.

Marland, M. (1986, Spring). Has the school library a future? *International Review of Children's Literature and Librarianship, 1*(1), 1-21.

Parker, A. (1986, Spring). New skills, new opportunities—the role of in-service training. *International Review of Children's Literature and Librarianship, 1*(1), 1-21.

Shepherd, J. (1986, Spring). A crisis of confidence: The future of children's work. *International Review of Children's Literature and Librarianship, 1*(1), 22-32.

Steinfirst, S. (1979). Education of the young adult librarian. In J. V. Rogers (Ed.), *Libraries and young adults: Media, services, and librarianship* (pp. 145-64). Littleton, CO: Libraries Unlimited.

Witucki, V. (1979). Another look at theory and practice in library education, and a proposal. In *Frontiers of library service for youth* (essays honoring Frances E. Henne) (pp. 116-24). New York: Columbia University, School of Library Service.

JOAN L. ATKINSON
Graduate School of Library Service
University of Alabama
Tuscaloosa, Alabama

Credentials, Competencies, and Certification

The process of licensing shapes the future of the profession by restricting entrance to those who meet certain qualifications. Licensing is a gatekeeping function, at least theoretically protecting the public from incompetent performance. Before we assess where we are and where we hope to be in relation to this topic, distinctions need to be made among terms.

Credentials is a general term indicating that the holder is duly entitled to claim a certain status. In librarianship, the M.L.S. degree is often held to be the requisite credential for entrance into the field. The term *competencies* is more specific, indicating a listing of abilities and skills, often task-oriented, that one should possess to be a good practitioner. *Certification* is an endorsement to practice in a specialized area, such as medical or school librarianship. While these terms apply to individuals, *accreditation* applies to educational programs which meet certain standards of quality and relevance in preparing future practitioners.

Accreditation of programs leading toward the M.L.S. degree is conferred by the American Library Association (ALA). Accreditation of the more narrowly-focused specialization of school librarianship is a function of the National Council on Accreditation of Teacher Education (NCATE) and, usually, a state department of education.

The current picture of licensing for the youth specialization is disparate and dismaying. Youth services librarians are separated into two distinct groups depending on the environment in which they work—i.e., school or public libraries. Factors related to their establishing competence to practice focus entirely on their environment rather than on skills and philosophies needed by all. There is virtually no licensing for public library youth specialists at the local level—only at systems or state levels and then only in certain states. When a credential is required, it is ordinarily the M.L.S. degree. The local public library, if it has a designated youth specialist at all, usually hires a person who likes children or young adults, is relatively outgoing and articulate, and will work for minimum wages or little more.

In the school setting, the certification required at entry level is generally the same as that for beginning teachers and it is determined state by state. The 1986-87 edition of *Requirements for Certification* (Burks, 1986) and the most recent compilation of this information in *School Library Journal* (Franklin, 1984) indicates that wide variation exists in courses of study, competency testing, level of certification, and nomenclature. To illustrate, fewer than half the states require a course in children's or young adult literature for certification. Twenty-three different titles are used for the school library media specialist. Fewer than ten states require a master's degree for initial certification.

The disheartening reality is that licensing practices for the youth specialization separate youth librarians from each other. Of equal importance, these practices cut them off from the rest of the field of librarianship, because youth librarians can be, and usually are, certified after completion of an undergraduate program. Other librarians generally begin to practice their craft after receiving an M.L.S. degree from a school accredited by the American Library Association. This important difference in educational preparation undoubtedly contributes to and exacerbates the feelings of isolation and inferiority repeatedly expressed by youth specialists (Ballett & Cornell, 1986).

Standards have traditionally been used to raise the level of service. They set a minimum level of support for materials, services, and personnel. Ideally, licensing is related directly or indirectly to these standards. Youth librarianship does have such standards, but for various reasons they have lost their power to effect improvements in service.

The most recent public library standards are a 1966 revision of standards published in 1956 that focused on development of county and regional library systems (ALA, 1967). Among the weaknesses charged to these standards are an emphasis on the institution rather than on services, on input rather than on output measures, lack of challenge for larger libraries but impossible expectations for small libraries, and requirements based on opinions of librarians rather than on solid research. These considerations plus other projects of the Public Library Association (PLA) during the early 1970s (Lynch, 1982) prepared the way for *A Planning Process for Public Libraries* (American Library Association, 1980), a document that represents a shift from a single national standard to locally-determined standards.

The manual provides guidelines to help libraries develop a set of standards that are appropriate for their community and which reflect their own philosophy. Since the delivery of this paper, new school library media standards have been published (ALA & AECT, 1988). The planning process has the advantage of involving local groups who will ultimately be responsible for funding but has the drawback of demanding time-consuming, external participation. Realistically, there are situations in which a local group simply cannot be sufficiently trained or committed to carry through an involved planning process. In these cases, standards structured at the national level could help to identify service goals for local libraries. Meanwhile, during the last few years, several states have developed standards or guidelines for services to youth—e.g., New York, Virginia, Illinois, and New Jersey (New York Library Association, 1984; Cram, 1984, p. 91; Illinois Library Association, 1981; New Jersey State Library, 1986). Their impact on services has yet to be assessed, but they offer models that can be used as ammunition by those in other states hoping to improve their own services.

In the school setting, the question of standards is a hotly debated issue this year. James Liesener, chairman of the American Association of School Librarians (AASL)/Association for Educational Communications and Technology (AECT) Standards Writing Committee, reported to the AASL Minneapolis Conference audience in September that his committee has an outline and schedule for their work that will permit a 1987 publication date for new school library standards (Flagg, 1986).

Of the three most recent sets of school library standards (1960, 1969, and 1975), those of 1960 are generally considered to have had the greatest impact and those of 1975 the least. Several factors account for the difference. The country's economic and social climate in 1960 was right for this project. A generous grant ($100,000) from the Council on Library Resources funded a dissemination and publicity campaign for the *1960 Standards*. The Knapp Foundation granted $1,130,000 to fund a nationwide demonstration project. A great deal of federal money was available and specifically earmarked for school library media programs. Many schools greatly expanded their programs to reflect the *1960 Standards* or created them where none had previously existed. The *1960 Standards* seemed attainable, where the 1975 ones did not. In materials, for example, the *1960 Standards* called for ten books per student, the *1969 Standards* mandated twenty books or audiovisual units, and the *1975 Standards* again doubled the figure, recommending forty items per student. Although the term *items* is sufficiently vague to permit some latitude in interpretation, meeting this standard would nevertheless have been difficult because funding for education since 1975 has been less abundant, and retrenchment has become the norm. One finds schools today whose programs do not even measure up to the *1960 Standards* in terms of resources or staffing. A handout distributed at AASL's Minneapolis conference highlighting the 1985-86 Survey of Public School Libraries and Media Centers, reported that 93 percent of public schools had media centers and that 79 percent were served by a certified library media specialist part of the time (AASL, 1986).

Another factor in the successful implementation of the *1960 Standards* and the somewhat less successful implementation of the *1969 Standards* was that persons important to their implementation were involved in their development. Representatives from approximately twenty education agencies, such as the Association for Supervision and Curriculum Development and the Department of Rural Education, were members of advisory committees. No doubt this involvement greatly aided in spreading the word and marshaling support for the two sets of standards. The *1975 Standards*, on the other hand, had no such advisory committee. Dissemination efforts were mostly restricted to prepublication announcements and postpublication critiques in library literature. These evaluations found the standards to be jargon-laden, vague, and incomprehensible. They did not receive endorsements by state boards of education and have been generally ignored by everyone except us.

So standards in general have reflected political realities; they have frequently failed as change agents. Perhaps improvement in the way standards are created might make them more effective, or perhaps it would help if someone had a vested interest in implementing them. Or perhaps standards are not the best means to bring about improvement in service; and while standards are necessary, they are not sufficient, certainly in relation to licensing.

There are two major problems with current licensing practices: (1) the process is not producing the kind of people doing the kinds of jobs we want; and (2) the process is not providing the numbers we need to fill existing positions. As to the first concern, we could all share horror stories, tales that we would like to think are exaggerated but know are not—e.g., the team of two school media specialists in one high school who spend six weeks of the school year doing nothing but writing overdue notices, who readily admit that they do nothing that could not be done as well by a bright tenth grader, and who don't care; the public library children's person whose goal (unstated but real) is never to have any item in the collection that could be offensive to anyone. Few would argue that youth librarianship in general has attracted capable, highly motivated practitioners. Ken Haycock (1985) said: "There are still too many teacher-librarians who are paid professional salaries for being effective homemakers, book exchangers, and all round martyrs" (p. 108). James Liesener (1985) also acknowledged that "we are having difficulty attracting the level of talent that we once did" (p. 17). Jane Hannigan (1984), writing in *Libraries and the Learning Society*, observed that: "As a field we seem to accept and tolerate a large measure of rank incompetence in practice" (p. 31).

Many factors contribute to the difficulty of attracting capable people to youth librarianship. Financial incentives are comparatively low, as are status and image. The workplace is often pervaded by infantilism, with little trust, respect, or autonomy bestowed on the youth specialist. Capable women and ethnic minorities now have options to enter fields formerly dominated by males and whites and are less likely to settle into education and librarianship. However, a greater hindrance is the fact that, especially for youth specialists in the school setting, there is no consensus within either the library or the school community what their roles should be. The professional literature, written mostly by library educators, overflows with convictions about proper roles. Haycock (1985) says: "The very nature of the role...is that of initiator and change agent" (p. 105). Liesener emphasizes the mediation function and views the youth specialist as an information intermediary. Unfortunately these terms do not communicate a clear message to prospective students or employers. Philip Turner (1985) has simplified the terminology and called his book on the role of the school library media specialist, *Helping Teachers Teach* (see also "Future of School Library Media Preparation," 1987).

When school principals do not know the potential of the school media program, and recent research documents the fact that they do not (Ballet & Cornell, 1986), failure is inevitable. The library may become the caretaker for students during the teachers' preparation periods, the repository for driver's education students who cannot all be out driving at one time, or the rainy day place for anyone who cannot be outside. Teachers, of course, conclude that the librarian as chief clerk has a soft job, and the youth specialist's image and status are encoded in stereotypic and stale jokes. Burnout and mediocrity follow rather naturally.

Evaluation practices contribute to another kind of failure. When basic competencies lists are compiled, items included too often fail to distinguish the librarian's role from the classroom teacher's role, and librarians fall into the trap of teaching hour after hour of library skills—in a vacuum, out of context, and useless for students' learning. Preparation programs also receive and deserve a great deal of the criticism for turning out youth specialists who either do not know or do not care what they are about.

The idea of listing basic competencies for the youth specialist and setting goals and measuring performance based on the list is not a bad idea. In fact, if a competency list goes beyond task orientation and includes attitudes and qualities of personality like empathy and caring, its use can be very helpful in establishing roles and scope of work for the youth specialist. The Young Adult Services Division (1982) list, "Competencies for Librarians Serving Youth," has this potential. It was developed originally to circulate among library school faculty, to encourage their developing or identifying courses that would help newly-graduated youth professionals to have the needed competencies. Happily, this listing has been found useful by practitioners. The New York Library Association's *Standards for Youth Services in Public Libraries of New York State* (1984) adapted it to include the entire spectrum of youth services and not just young adult services.

The second problem, that of numbers, is also difficult. Some preparation programs put a great deal of energy into thinking through the kind of people they are training and the curriculum they offer, only to have the system subverted when demand exceeds supply. In a crunch—and we always seem to be in a crunch—exceptions to the credentialing system are made. Poorly-trained and unmotivated people are placed in positions they will cling to for the rest of their lives.

Rectifying the situation requires a realistic appraisal of the financial resources that are likely to be available. The theory of wages that our society has adopted is one that pays handsomely for the professions of medicine, law, and business on the grounds that medicine protects our life, law protects our property, and business creates jobs for other people. Other societies may have similar priorities but allocate resources differently to reach these goals. For example, an allergy-sufferer in this country consulted a physician who tested her for fifty-two allergies and designed a shot uniquely for her. When she moved to England, her physician, without any pretesting, administered a standard shot covering the three most common allergies. It worked and no further testing was presumed necessary. When the Chinese in the 1960s asked the question, How shall we improve the health of our people? the answer was the training of a core of medical technicians called barefoot doctors who could treat and restore health to a high percentage of those who were ill.

Our society is apparently unwilling to increase substantially the funding for education and librarianship. Hence we need to ask the following questions. How can resources be allocated differently to provide a more productive environment for both children and young adults and the youth librarians who serve them? How can the licensing process be altered to effect this needed reallocation?

In my opinion the report of The Holmes Group (1986), *Tomorrow's Teachers*, a plan for the reform of teacher education, provides a model which youth librarianship could profitably consider. The Holmes Group realized that reforming teacher education involves not only colleges of education but many others—i.e., the undergraduate programs of colleges and universities, the schools in which teachers work, state departments of education which license teachers, and society's willingness to pay for improved teaching. The Holmes Group recommendation related to licensing is that a differentiated staffing pattern be established which licenses at the instructor, professional teacher, and career professional teacher levels. The latter two credentials require preparation at the graduate level plus demonstration of effective practice. They are considered professional certifications and are renewable and tenure-earning. The former requires preparation at the undergraduate level and passing examinations which test subject-matter competence. It is not considered a professional certification, is not renewable or tenure-earning, and does not permit the bearer to practice autonomously but only to work under the supervision of a career professional teacher. The reward structure would also be differentiated monetarily and also in number of opportunities to engage in a variety of workday activities commensurate with skill, preparation, and interest.

Adapting this model to youth librarianship would involve changes in many details. A differentiated licensing pattern would, however, recognize and appropriately reward different levels of commitment, preparation, and activity. In the school setting the instructor librarian would have an undergraduate major and tested subject-matter competence in one of the disciplines of the sciences, social sciences, or humanities. Working under the supervision of a career professional librarian, the instructor librarian would carry on a number of activities—e.g., some clerical (keeping circulation records), some managerial (supervising student assistants), some related to reading motivation (reading aloud, storytelling, booktalking), some to teaching (how to use indexes).

The professional librarian would, in addition to satisfying the instructor-level requirements, also have a master's degree in librarianship and would have passed an intellectually defensible competency examination in that area. The professional librarian would function independently and would both conduct learning activities with students and consult with teachers, other support staff, and administrators to plan and design instructional units. The career professional librarian would have demonstrated effective performance at the professional librarian level. Through a combination of further education and identification of interest and ability in a specialized area—such as supervising instructors or practicum students, carrying on research, participating with a university in training librarians—the career professional librarian would demonstrate ability to work in positions of authority in both the library and the school. Activities of the career professional librarian would emphasize the advocacy role and include contacts with students, teachers, administrators, universities, state departments of education, and other community and professional policy-making groups.

One of the advantages of a differentiated licensing process is its ability to respond to the disequilibrium between supply and demand. At present, shortages in qualified personnel result in lowering standards and admitting the poorly-trained to permanent positions. The differentiated pattern would allow filling vacancies at the instructor level. If the person hired wished to become a professional, there would be a period of years during which the appropriate training could take place. If the person did not make a commitment to the profession, the certificate would expire after five years and employment would be terminated. Taxpayers might be spared some expensive mistakes. The process also has the potential to encourage commitment to and investment in the profession by talented persons who desire some occupational mobility and choice. Their expanded career opportunities and rewards would cut down on the tendency to settle into boredom or unexamined routines and would provide incentives for continued growth and development of diverse interests.

In the public library setting the differentiated licensing pattern would need to take into account the size, demography, and funding of the local public library plus other factors related to public library development. It is nevertheless desirable for the Public Library Association in cooperation with the Association for Library Service to Children and the Young Adult Services Division—all divisions of the American Library Association—to formulate a differentiated credentialing process that recognizes current reality and at the same time challenges communities to improve youth services. The professional certification for children's or young adult librarians should continue to be the M.L.S. degree, as Perritt and Heim (1987) have reiterated persuasively. For those individuals for whom this certification is impossible to acquire, or for those communities who cannot afford to pay for the professional certification, there needs to be an equivalent to the barefoot doctor training and certification. (I hesitate to call this the barefoot youth specialist certification, though the nomenclature may fit the salary scale!) Some service is preferable to no service for young people who live in rural, small, or poor communities (Vavrek, 1982).

Conclusion

Two major problems affect current licensing practices for youth librarians:
1. The process has not produced the kind of people doing the kind of jobs that are needed.
2. The process has not provided the numbers needed to fill existing positions.

Solutions to these problems cannot address the licensing process alone; they must involve a systems approach, analyzing the total environment in which youth specialists work. Licensing is influenced by preparation programs, accrediting agencies, state boards of education, state law, national standards, success or failure of those already licensed, the workplace, research, and costs at all levels.

The actions that could result in more effective credentialing practices are as multifaceted as the problems. These are:
1. Develop national and state standards or guidelines for youth services in both school and public libraries. These documents must articulate

clearly what the program of services intends to accomplish and what roles the youth librarian needs to assume. These documents must eschew obfuscation. They must be straightforward and free of jargon so that we can coalesce around them and use them to spread the word to the uninformed or uncommitted.

2. Examine ways to improve the quality of the product—i.e., the youth librarian. This examination should include scrutiny of what goes into the training process (input measures) and what is produced (output measures). Accreditation practices should screen programs and function as a gatekeeper at the input level. Competency testing at the output stage should assure the individual's achievement of a minimum level of knowledge and expertise.

   Is there a way to toughen the accreditation requirements for programs that train youth librarians without raising the cost of accreditation to an exorbitant level? Single-purpose programs that train school library media specialists range from the poorest to the best available preparation. Should ALA or AASL be responsible for accreditation of these programs rather than NCATE, or should ALA/AASL investigate ways to participate in the NCATE accreditation reviews?[1] How can ALA's own Committee on Accreditation (COA) be persuaded to scrutinize more closely the quality of training youth specialists receive in general-purpose ALA-accredited M.L.S. programs? Is an attempt to get more youth librarians appointed to COA site visitation teams worth the effort involved?

   Competency testing has often been a joke, failing to discriminate between the fit and the unfit. A highly charged political issue, it has unfortunately pitted professional educators against state government officials over who shall determine the proper credentials for those entering the profession (*The Alabama Librarian*, 1982, p. 4). With appropriate research applied to test construction and validation, however, the adequacy and fairness of such tests could be established, and they could contribute to protecting the public from an inferior product.

3. Work toward a differentiated staffing and licensing pattern that obviates the current practice of hiring poorly trained personnel for permanent positions when demand exceeds supply. The Holmes Group report, *Tomorrow's Teachers*, may serve as a model because: (a) it is relatively free of professional jargon and communicates to an educated reader from any discipline; and (b) there are many parallels between teaching and youth librarianship, including generally low professional status and image, licensing at the undergraduate level, and the importance of youth advocacy.

4. Speak with a strong, unified voice from national professional

associations, especially among the three youth divisions of the American Library Association.

Issues related to licensing persons to practice a profession that affects the public good are inevitably complex and confounding. Licensing for youth librarianship fits the pattern. The future is likely to present a labyrinth, not a paved highway for our convenience. Like Theseus in the labyrinth of the Cretan King Minos, we need courage, imagination, shrewd planning, and belief in ourselves if we are to be victorious. The three youth divisions of the American Library Association are poised to adventure, accepting the ambiguities of the task, and hanging on, as Theseus did to Ariadne's thread, for dear life.

NOTES

American Association of School Librarians. (1986). *Highlights of the 1985-86 survey of public school libraries and media centers-early tabulations*. Chicago: ALA.

American Association of School Librarians and Association for Educational Communications and Technology. (1975). *Media programs: District and School*. Chicago: ALA.

American Library Association. American Association of School Librarians. (1960). *Standards for school library programs*. Chicago: ALA.

American Library Association and National Education Association. (1969). *Standards for school media programs*. Chicago: ALA.

American Library Association. Public Library Association. (1967). *Minimum standards for public library systems, 1966*. Chicago: ALA, PLA.

Ballet, R. M., & Cornell, R. A. (1986). Professionalizing our profession: Twentieth-century countdown. In S. L. Aaron & P. R. Scales (Eds.), *School library media annual 1986* (pp. 173-82). Littleton, CO: Libraries Unlimited.

Burks, M. P. (1986). *Requirements for certification for elementary schools, secondary schools, junior colleges* (51st Ed.). Chicago: University of Chicago Press.

Cram, L. (1984, Fall). Young adult services guidelines for Virginia. *Public Libraries, 23*, 91.

Flagg, G. (1986, November). Standards status. *American Libraries, 17*, 740.

Franklin, A. Y. (1984, January). School library media certification requirements: 1984 update. *School Library Journal, 30*, 23-28.

Hannigan, J. A. (1984). Vision to purpose to power: A quest for excellence in the education of library and information science professionals. In *Libraries and the learning society: Papers in response to "A nation at risk"* (pp. 22-62). Chicago: American Library Association.

Haycock, K. (1985, Spring). Strengthening the foundations for teacher-librarianship. *School Library Media Quarterly, 13*, 102-109.

The Holmes Group. (1986). *Tomorrow's teachers*. East Lansing, MI: The Holmes Group.

Illinois Library Association. Children's Librarians Section. (1981). *Foundations of quality: Guidelines for public library service to children*. Chicago: Illinois Library Association.

Liesener, J. W. (1985, Fall). Learning at risk: School library media programs in an information world. *School Library Media Quarterly, 14*, 11-20.

Lynch, M. J. (1982). The Public Library Association and public library planning. *Journal of Library Administration, 2*, 30-40.

New Jersey State Library. Children's Services in Public Libraries. Guidelines Committee. (1986). *Guidelines for children's services in public libraries of New Jersey*. Trenton, NJ: New Jersey State Library.

New York Library Association. (1984). *Standards for youth services in public libraries in New York State*. New York: New York Library Association, Task Force on Standards for Youth Services, Youth Services Section.

Perritt, P. H., & Heim, K. M. (1987, Winter). ALA-accredited master's degree: Considerations for youth services librarianship. *Top of the News, 43*.

Turner, P. M. (1985). *Helping teachers teach.* Littleton, CO: Libraries Unlimited.

Vavrek, B. (1982, April). Profession needs a new entry level: Non-MLS workers in rural libraries are isolated from the mainstream. *American Libraries, 13*, 271-272.

Young Adult Services Division. Education Committee. (1982, September). Competencies for librarians serving youth. *School Library Journal, 29*, 51.

FOOTNOTES

1. The Fall 1984 issue of the *Journal of Education for Library and Information Science* reports the proceedings of a 1984 ALISE conference, which was devoted to the topic of accreditation. Whether ALA should accredit programs other than those leading to the M.L.S. degree was one of the many questions considered. The tremendous costs involved in accreditation no doubt deter ALA from broadening its current accreditation program.

2. Alabama is one of the states which has had a bitter confrontation over this question. See *The Alabama Librarian*, November 1982, p. 4, and September 1983, p. 1 for details.

JANA VARLEJS

Director, Professional Development Studies
School of Communication, Information & Library Studies
Rutgers, The State University of New Jersey

Continuing Education: Providing for Change, Renewal, and Growth

Why should this Allerton Institute on library services for children and young adults include a session on continuing education (CE)? Are there different issues and problems associated with CE for youth services librarians than for librarians in general? If so, what are they? The task today is to explore these questions, to identify the concerns about CE, and, if agreement is reached on some specific conclusions, to contribute to the "Youth Agenda" which will be formulated at the conclusion of the conference.

From the perspective of one who administers a continuing education program which seeks to serve professionals in all types of libraries, media, and information centers, one answer to the questions just posed is no—the basic issues and problems relating to continuing education are not very different, whether one is talking about school librarians or directors of public libraries or online searchers in industry. There are differences in degree, however, and therefore the answer to the question, should we be talking about CE for youth librarians specifically, is yes. In fact, a case can be made to support the contention that youth librarians are singularly disadvantaged in regard to continuing education.

What are the problems which seem to be pervasive and to cut across types of positions and libraries? When looking at the complaints people have about continuing education, they really come from two categories of complainers. The first is a group that could be called the consumer—individuals who have an interest in their own professional development but have difficulty finding learning opportunities that match their needs and expectations. They complain—with justification—that it is hard to discover what is being offered, that little of what can be identified is relevant to their particular need at that moment, that much of what is available is superficial or poorly done, that the cost in time and money is too high, and that the encouragement and rewards that ought to accrue to the CE participant are not forthcoming.

The second group of complainers comprises a motley assemblage of CE providers, library administrators, educators, and professional profession-watchers who—again with considerable justification—blame the would-be or should-be CE consumers for failing to make enough of an effort to seek out learning opportunities, to take responsibility for their own learning, to be discriminating in their selection of CE activities, to play the Typhoid Mary role—as Regina Minudri calls it—by sharing what has been learned with colleagues back home, and especially for failing to demonstrate on the job that CE can make a difference in performance and ultimately in the quality of service for the library user.

Sometimes it seems that the profession is content with this standoff, with each camp feeling it has accomplished something by diagnosing the problem and pointing the finger at the other side. To be fair, during the last ten years there has been progress in recognizing the importance of providing for CE within the overall system of planning for the development of libraries and librarianship. Many states have included CE in statewide planning. The Continuing Library Education Network and Exchange (CLENE) has created much greater awareness of and has facilitated communication and support for CE. It has worked to improve CE by developing criteria for quality and a voluntary provider approval system. ALA's Committee on Library Education (SCOLE) has recently established a CE subcommittee, which is cooperating with CLENE (now a round table of ALA) in an effort to have ALA approve the CLENE CE quality criteria as ALA guidelines. SCOLE is working to improve headquarters' support for an association-wide CE role. Such support could help AASL, ALSC, and YASD to serve better the CE needs of their members.

In an article which will be published in the forthcoming Winter issue of *Top of the News* (Varlejs, 1987), it is argued that the ALA youth divisions should be doing much more in the area of continuing education, but that they cannot do what is needed without help from the association as a whole. In order to get help, they will have to form a coalition and fight for it.

Very briefly, this is the argument. Despite the good job the divisions do with offering programming at conferences, the impact is not very great because few practioners attend, at least relative to their total numbers. Publications, cassettes, and now videotapes reach a wider audience and are enormously useful in helping librarians to keep up to date and to continue learning at their own pace at little cost and inconvenience. Praiseworthy as all these services are, however, they fall far short of what should be available considering the great number of things a youth services librarian needs to know and do. Moreover, the disparity in basic preparation is quite large, and therefore one has to keep in mind the needs of practitioners who have few, if any, courses in materials and library services for youth. This is not as serious a problem for school as for public librarians—because of certification requirements—but there is still enormous variation in the entry-level preparation. In New Jersey, for example, it is possible to be certified as an educational media specialist—i.e., school librarian—if one has a masters in educational media. Most of the people who hold this degree have never had a course in cataloging nor in children's literature.

In addition to these remedial and survival CE needs, there is a third level which might be called the parachute category. Career ladders for youth librarians are limited, but there are some rungs which allow increased responsibility without having to leave the specialty—positions such as system or regional coordinator or consultant (which require a new set of skills).

Given these several categories and different levels, not to mention the considerable overlap with education and with child and adolescent development, listing all the knowledge, skill, and attitude areas that CE for youth services librarians ought to cover becomes a formidable task. If one did take a few weeks to develop the list and then matched it against what is actually being offered—not just by ALA but throughout the country by local associations, state library agencies, library schools, and other providers—one would end up with a very lopsided list. Judging from calendars of events published in some of the widely read journals, most CE identified as designed for youth services librarians is either book or microcomputer oriented.

What is available, or at least that which is easily identified as available, simply is not enough. There is very little on planning or evaluating services, on child or adolescent development, on managing a school library or public library youth services department in a retrenchment era, on how children process information, or on the role of reading in an electronic age.

In this last statement is the implication that knowledge of how children process information, for example, is indeed important for youth services librarians, and that it therefore constitutes a CE need. How can one say that? Has there been a valid and reliable study of a randomly selected sample of practitioners? No, but it is possible to perceive the increasing interest in children's information processing by browsing through the literature, talking with people, attending conferences, and keeping an eye on what is going on in the world at large to note new ideas and social phenomena which might have implications for librarians. These are legitimate ways for a CE provider to do CE needs assessment. It is not scientific and rigorous, but it does keep one alert to the changing environment so that needs can be anticipated and new learning activities can be ready at the moment that a particular need is just beginning to crystallize. It is a way of trying to nudge the profession forward, to help it be proactive rather than merely reactive.

But this way of doing CE needs assessment by hunch should never stand alone—it should supplement the basic and most essential kinds of needs assessment that each librarian must do for herself, using the best available checklists of competencies for the position she holds. The school library field has the Case and Lowrey *Behavioral Requirements Analysis Checklist* (Case, 1973); YASD has produced a list of competencies for YA librarians (American Library Association, 1982); and the New York Library Association has adapted the YASD list so that children's librarians can also use it (Young, 1985). In this regard, the youth services library field is ahead of most of the profession.

However, as suggested at the outset, youth librarians can be seen as suffering certain disadvantages in continuing their education. As has already been concluded, what is offered does not match the range of needs. Not mentioned as yet are the problems caused by the relative isolation of youth services librarians, and the effect this has on their ability to take strong action to improve their access to appropriate CE. For the most part, the school librarian is the only librarian in his/her school, and often in his/her town. This is certainly also true of the children's librarian. As for the YA librarian, if there is one, she or he probably is the only one of the species for many miles around. In the typical situation, there are not enough people to form the sized group which makes the traditional workshop or short course format viable. Self-assessment and self-directed learning are almost the only routes available.

On the other hand, because they have made good progress toward identifying the competencies required for their specialties, youth services librarians are in a good position to define the content of the CE "curriculum" which they need. In addition, because they know that their colleagues throughout the country are often isolated from their peers and from professional support groups, underpaid and overworked, they can be quite confident in recommending that this curriculum needs to be very portable, flexible, and affordable. It will not do much good if it is offered once a year in Chicago or wherever ALA is meeting. This curriculum must be available on loan, in formats varied to suit the topic and different individual learning styles, paced for self-study but adaptable for small groups, geared to beginners as well as advanced learners.

If one thinks about what it would take to develop this kind of "mail-order" CE, it has to be admitted that it would require a very large investment in resources to develop and maintain. No single state library agency, library school, state professional association, or ALA division by itself is likely to have the staff and money required. If the profession really wants this kind of program, a way to pool resources has to be found. ALA is the only organization which is big enough to harbor such an effort. The youth services divisions of ALA have usually felt themselves to be underdogs within the ALA power structure. This need not be the case if they form a strong alliance and work toward specific objectives which will benefit the profession at large as well as youth services. Working for an agenda that calls for stronger support from the organization for the CE efforts of the divisions seems be an effective way to exercise some clout to good effect.

Summary/Recommendations

The idea of mail-order CE has potential for alleviating the inadequate supply of CE for youth services librarians. It is felt, however, that interaction is essential, and that solitary self-directed learning cannot be the only mode. A great deal is gained from discussion with others in groups. Uses of new technology to bridge distance and permit interaction should be explored.

ALA should experiment with several learning packages to test the response. There should be programs for paraprofessionals as well as for professionals. A possible model might be the learning modules recently developed for staff training in the Area 2 Library Services Authority in Indiana. Another model is the CE course by Jane Robbins-Carter and Douglas Zweizig which ran in *American Libraries* from October 1985 through February 1986.

In addition to the facilitating of programs and packages, ALA should ensure better communication and an enlarged clearinghouse function for CE. There should be more exchange of information about existing programs and resources which could be shared if people knew about them.

NOTES

American Library Association. Young Adult Services Division. Education Committee. (1982, September). Young adults deserve the best: Competencies for librarians serving youth. *School Library Journal, 29,* 51.

Case, R. N., & Lowrey, A. M. (1973). *Behavioral requirements analysis checklist: A compilation of competency-based job functions and task statements for school library media personnel.* Chicago: American Library Association.

Varlejs, J. (1987, Winter). Continuing education for youth services librarians: A diagnosis and prescription. *Top of the News, 43,* 193-202.

Young, D. (1985, Spring). Standards for the library, for the librarian. *Public Libraries, 24,* 30-31.

MARGARET MARY KIMMEL

University of Pittsburgh
School of Library and Information Science
Pittsburgh, Pennsylvania

Halos and Pitchforks: Questions about Librarians Serving Youth

All occupations are worthy of study, a fact documented by many since Robert Park's classic research on the hobo, the taxi-dance-hall girl, and the professional thief. Librarianship, too, has been subjected to in-depth analysis on everything from the personality of the librarian to questions about the attributes of the profession. The subspecialty of work with young people has recently been subjected to much scrutiny, primarily because there is such a need for specialists in schools and public libraries at the entry level.

Some claim that this shortage is due to a failure of professional education. Others point to low pay and lower status accorded to those who work with children. Both factors are undoubtedly significant, but some others, such as job satisfaction, should be considered. Whether sorting clay tablets or entering items onto OCLC, it has always been the librarian's belief that the job being done was important. Preserving the culture, offering the great works of literature to the masses, or organizing the contributions of Fred Rogers have been tasks in which one could take some pride. But now there would appear to be some confusion about those tasks and just how meaningful they are, especially as they relate to young people.

Another consideration may be related to the changing role of women in society at large. Because organizational patterns in schools and public libraries are shifting, fewer managerial positions are provided within the subspecialty. This is occurring at a time when women are selecting more diversified occupational choices within and outside of librarianship.

These and other questions need study as we consider directions that information service to young people might take. It is the purpose of this discussion to explore some of the issues which affect the provision of such service. Are there factors within the profession which are drawing entry level individuals to other service areas? Is it a crisis at the entry level only or are other aspects of the service also in trouble? What are the social issues beyond those of professional concern affecting this subspecialty?

Other Professional Subspecialties

Career patterns of women in a variety of occupational groups provide interesting but inconclusive evidence about their provision of service to young people. It is predicted that by 1990 at least "75 percent of children will have both parents working outside the home" (Brazelton, 1985, p. xviii). Now the working woman has a choice of occupations far broader than the traditional "feminized professions." Other occupational opportunities may have drawn away potential candidates from a predominately female subspecialty like service to children.

In law, for instance, family law practice draws many women. Of the Family Law Section of the American Bar Association, 26 percent are female, a fact consistent with the "widely held opinion that female lawyers tend to concentrate in those fields of law dealing with the problems of individuals" (Smith, 1983, p. 241). Furthermore, women are more likely to hold positions outside the private practice of law and, therefore, are less likely to be associated with law firms of any size.

In medicine, pediatrics has long been the favored specialty of women medical graduates. In a recent study of specialty preferences at five medical schools, males had higher preferences for high risk procedures and patients at risk while women students scored higher in a preference for handling preventive care and patient responsibility and participation. Of the six major medical subspecialties, the top three choices for women were: (1) ob/gyn, (2) pediatrics, and (3) internal medicine. For men the choices were: (1) internal medicine, (2) family practice, and (3) surgery (Cuca, 1979, p. 429). Implications of these and several other studies suggest that the recent influx of women has not substantially altered career patterns of physicians.

Women in medicine with home and family responsibilities are more likely to choose subspecialties which relate to their identification as nurturer as well as healer. These subspecialties often have distinctions in such areas as hours of service and salary that are markedly different. Pediatricians, for instance, in 1984 earned less than half of what anesthesiologists did. In the years between 1974 and 1984, salaries of psychiatrists doubled while pediatricians showed only about a 5 percent increase in income. The only subspecialty with more patient contact hours per week is family/general practice (Reynolds & Duann, 1985, pp. 60, 70, 123). These differences, however, are true for both male and female pediatricians and may reflect more about the status of the client than the gender of the pediatrician.

In the ministry, the role of women is even more controversial. In an article in the *Journal of Public and International Affairs*, the Rev. Beryl Choi (1983) states unequivocally:

> Although female members far outnumber males in the Christian Church, though for thousands of years women have been the nurturing foundation of their people—the very essence of community—they have been, in that community of religious faith, a disenfranchised group. The barriers to power and prestige for women in the Church, though not absolute, are certainly ubiquitous and ancient. (p. 33)

Women in many of the Christian churches have been relegated to the role of educator with little voice in policy and certainly no voice in theology. The role of religious educator is a significant one, but in terms of growth and change, a lack of involvement in policy and theology may restrict development. In the first decade of the twentieth century, 8 million immigrants landed at Ellis Island, many of them Roman Catholics. The education provided for many of these new arrivals was developed by a cadre of religious who were "the sacrificial and hidden asset of the whole system" (Hesburg, 1986, p. 161). The only words more frequently heard than "Look it up in the card catalog" were "but Sister said." Yet today, vocations in the religious orders are down and many regard church schools as merely a relatively inexpensive private school rather than a religious educational experience.

What do these questions about the role of women in the traditional professions have to do with information services for young people? Perhaps the most significant factor is that librarianship is not alone in wondering where to find new recruits for new services. Many other occupational groups have difficulty identifying entry level professionals for public service jobs dealing with youth. With the choice of careers more diversified for women, there are questions about the value placed on those occupations dealing with children and young people. Even larger questions relate to the value placed on the children themselves, who serves them, and who sets the policies that regulate the services.

The second major factor in the development of a cadre of trained professionals working with young people deals with the nature and philosophy of those agencies providing the service. It is here that school and public library people should be drawing together. Both institutions operate in the public, not-for-profit sector vying with other agencies battling for limited money to provide essential services. Instead, cooperative efforts often go astray. Networks exclude one or the other; territorial squabbles occupy time that would be better spent on work with young people. The current fuss about what age group is served by which division in the American Library Association is an example of such behavior.

The shifts in organizational structure in both schools and public

libraries also affect youth services specialists. The generalist approach
provided some children's and young adult librarians with opportunities to
advance as "program specialists" or "information managers." The
approach, however, often failed to provide the entry-level positions which
led to the cadre of specialists able and willing to transfer their skills from
dealing with children to dealing with board members or city managers. In
schools, many middle managers have also been eliminated. This not only
affects programs, creating a situation where there is no direction or planning, but it also means that, to advance, there is no place to go but out of
the service.

Librarians Serving Youth

Several studies recently have been conducted examining aspects of
education and the new professional. Both Fasick (1986, p. 613) and
Immroth (1987, p. 210) have considered the entry level professional and
found that, in general, most people in library school have some kind of
library work experience. While this makes classroom participation lively
("We do it this way in my library"), it may also mean that we are not
recruiting widely enough. A typical career pattern follows an individual
from page to clerk to library school. Incoming M.L.S. students at the University of Pittsburgh report an average of three years of library work experience before graduate school.

There is another problem in "growing" replacements. The library
profession has approximately 12 percent minority professionals in public
libraries (Guy, 1986, p. 5). As population shifts occur and minorities
become in fact majorities, there are fewer and fewer professionals to serve as
role models. Although a study of population growth indicates a strong
increase in the number of black and Hispanic children, there is no indication of a similar growth in numbers of black and Hispanic librarians.

On the other hand, there is strong evidence that many people who
work with children do not have *any* professional education. In a survey of
children's librarians just released by the Library Research Center at the
University of Illinois, 88 percent of the sample had some college education,
but only 50 percent had any library education. Less than half of the 50
percent had completed the M.L.S. (Roy, 1986, p. 47). These figures are
substantiated by preliminary results of a study of Pennsylvania librarians
serving children which indicates that outside of metropolitan systems, it is
likely that a volunteer or clerk will be providing service to children.

More than half of the public libraries in the United States serve
populations under 10,000. These small rural libraries usually have some
kind of service for children and young people but with little quality
control. Collections are poorly maintained and "craft programs" abound.

The profession must wrestle with the question of whether to write off such efforts and worry only about "professional service" or take the responsibility for including those who will never get a graduate degree. Continuing education programs that offer *only* the practice and not one whit of philosophy of service perpetuate the system.

Libraries without youth specialists who have the first professional degree are not confined to rural areas, however. In tight times, administrators often felt they were unable to afford expensive professionals to work with children and young people. College graduates (or even those with less education) were hired to fill vacancies and cut down on personnel costs. Some major city systems have begun to build back their professional staff, but the process is a long one. Advertisements for children's librarians are widely circulated, but the role models aren't there. Neither are the new children's librarians.

Many have voiced concern over the failure of library schools to provide faculty and courses in services to children. It is true that some schools have dropped such specializations. But higher education, especially professional education, is market driven. When the demand for courses is present, the courses are offered. Information is big business and provides a seemingly endless job market for today's pragmatic student. The demand for courses and even a shift in the curriculum from one dominated by public libraries and public schools to one reflecting largely private sector employment is the result of many factors, not the least of which is student demand.

It is unrealistic to assume that higher education administrators are any more altruistic or high minded than their counterparts in the corporate world. Providing the professionals to work with children and young people in schools and public libraries is costly and time consuming, carries little status, and provides few millionaire alumni. Furthermore, it is hard to find qualified faculty to teach, research, and serve the community. There are relatively few children's specialists in doctorate programs around the country. The time is past when one's reputation alone will provide a tenured slot in a school of library and information science. Those individuals who are already a part of faculties need all our help and support. They need to be invited to give formal papers at conferences. They need the cooperation of libraries to act as field sites for their research. They need recognition by their peers in the field because it is lonely in that ivory tower where the only thing that colleagues agree on is a concern over parking.

Conclusion

Being a youth services specialist, however, still has its rewards. The children are responsive, even starved for stories. We have more media and materials available. Technology can enhance the richness of color in picture books and provide your favorite encyclopedia on a video disc. The job is challenging and exciting—and not very well paid.

Job satisfaction is, of course, tied to more than salary. There is a need for growth in responsibility and scope. For some youth service librarians there is a perceived lack of opportunity, however. Librarians report that they not only view the job as "dead-end" but feel unqualified for further responsibility. This perception is contradicted by reports which indicate that managerial skills *are* transferable and that controlling preschoolers at a story hour is related to working with a board of trustees, at least to some degree. Furthermore, many middle and upper level administrators in public library systems began as youth services specialists. State librarians, library directors, even university professors and deans began their careers by lighting candles at story hours and designing summer reading certificates and talking to local PTAs.

These problems at the entry level present a challenge to those engaged in this business of putting children and ideas and learning and reading together. There are societal concerns that deal with the status of our group as a female intensive occupation. Internally, the profession is in the midst of a profound realignment. Many are struggling to protect the right of citizens to information access in a society that sees information as a commodity. Children and their needs are often marginalized or so rigidly proscribed that professional growth is stifled. Yet we are intrigued by the potential of our work. Our job satisfaction comes from knowing that the job we do does make a difference. The communication of that satisfaction should be wider than the staff room discussion of what went on at story hour. We need to mount an active, vigorous recruitment effort, directed especially at minorities.

We need to look carefully at the continuing education activities provided by professional associations as well as colleges and universities. Meeting the creators of words and pictures is entertaining, sometimes enlightening, but should not be the extent of our efforts. We must provide opportunities to debate the direction of the service we provide, to consider the philosophy behind what we do.

Finally, it is significant to note that in the Illinois study, 97 percent of the respondents declared that if they had to start over, they would choose the same job again (Roy, 1986, p. 63). Professional problems abound, but interest and commitment is evident. Librarians who work with young people should be awarded halos not pitchforks.

NOTES

American Library Association. Office of Library Personnel Resources. (1986). *Academic and public librarians: Data by race, ethnicity and sex.* Chicago: ALA.

Brazelton, T. B. (1985). *Working and caring.* Reading, MA: Addison-Wesley.

Choi, B. T. (1982, Fall/Winter). Power and religion: The institutional church. *Journal of Public and International Affairs, 3,* 33.

Cuca, J. M. (1979, November). The specialization and career preferences of women and men recently graduated from U.S. medical schools. *Journal of the American Medical Women's Association, 34,* 429.

Fasick, A. (1986, Spring). Library and information science students. *Library Trends, 34*(4), 607-622.

Hesburg, T. M. (1986, October 4). Catholic education in America. *America, 155,* 161.

Immroth, B. (1987, Winter). Repopulating an endangered species: The issues and literature of recruitment. *Top of the News, 43*(2), 206-216.

Reynolds, R., & Duann, D. J. (Eds.). (1985). *Socioeconomic characteristics of medical practice, 1985.* Chicago: American Medical Association.

Roy, L. (1986, October). A survey of children's librarians in Illinois public libraries. *Illinois Library and Information Statistical Report No. 21.* Urbana-Champaign, IL: University of Illinois, Graduate School of Library and Information Science.

Smith, K.; Troha, M.; et al. (1983, Fall). A survey of the membership of the ABA section of family law. *Family Law Quarterly, 17,* 24.

HELEN LLOYD SNOKE

School of Library Science
University of Michigan
Ann Arbor, Michigan

What Library Schools Offer that School Library Media Specialists and Youth Services Librarians Need

When asked to speak at this conference on the topic, "What Library Schools Offer that School Library Media Specialists and Youth Services Librarians Need," it was decided that personal experience needed to be supplemented with curriculum revision at Michigan and with the rather sketchy knowledge of what some colleagues at other universities are doing in library education for youth services with current information from other programs. Many library school catalogs, including Michigan's, did not reflect the most recent developments, and the professional literature seemed to focus more on what is not being done rather than what is being done.

An urgent plea along with a brief questionnaire, "Educational Programs for Librarians Who Work With Youth," was sent in September 1986 to a representative of each U.S. institutional member of the Association of Library and Information Science Educators (ALISE). Both regular and associate members were included in the survey. In most cases the representatives were persons designated as having graduate specializations in library service for children and young adults and/or school library media programs, as reported in the *Journal of Education for Library and Information Science* directory issue, 1985-86. In spite of the short time frame and busy schedules, fifty-two of the seventy institutions contacted (74 percent) sent responses. Findings are presented in Table 1.

Table 1 shows that forty-nine of the fifty-two institutions responding (94 percent) have curriculum plans or concentrations for those preparing at the graduate level to be school library media specialists. Forty-one (79 percent) reported having curriculum plans or concentrations for youth services in public libraries. One might wonder whether failure to respond meant that those institutions do not have programs in either of these areas.

TABLE 1
INSTITUTIONS WITH GRADUATE PROGRAMS FOR YOUTH SERVICES

	Have		Do Not Have	
	Number	*Percentage*	*Number*	*Percentage*
School Library Media Curriculum Plan	49	94	3	6
Public Library Youth Services Curric. Plan	41	79	11	21

N = 52 Institutions

That should not be assumed, however. Several are known to have specializations in school library media and/or in public library services for youth and have faculty who have expertise in these fields.

Fifty institutions answered questions on number of faculty, full and part time, who teach courses related to library services for youth in school or public libraries. The number of full-time faculty reported ranges from zero to seven, and for part-time faculty, from zero to twenty. No institution reported zero for both full- and part-time faculty. Whether or not they have concentrations in youth services, all institutions represented in the survey have one or more faculty members with expertise in this field. Although two of the respondents stated philosophical commitments to adjunct faculty who are library practitioners, many others seemed to prefer a balance between full-time faculty who have the responsibility to develop curriculum, conduct research, and counsel students as well as to teach, and the practitioner or doctoral student with recent experience in the field.

Forty-four institutions responded to the question: Approximately what percent of those who graduated from your program within the past two years have been employed in public library youth services or in school library media programs? The range was 5 percent to 100 percent with a mean percentage of 40.7. The median was 30 percent and responses were tri-modal (10, 30, and 33 percent). However, if the eight institutions which are virtually single purpose (those reporting that 90 percent or more of their graduates have been placed in school or public library youth services positions) were excluded, the mean for the remaining thirty-six would be 28.4 percent and the median would be 26.5 percent. For a majority of library schools responding, more than one-fourth of their graduates have been placed in school or public library youth services positions within the past two years.

Program requirements, in addition to the courses required for all graduates, differ from one institution to another, but there are consistent strands to be found. For school library media concentrations, administration of media programs; literature or materials for children and young adults (sometimes with several courses specified in this area); the teaching or curriculum role of the library media specialist; design, production, and use of audiovisual media; computer literacy; and a practicum were often cited.

For a concentration in public library youth services, the number of required courses is usually less although library programs and services for children and young adults, literature or materials for children and young adults (several courses may be specified in this area), and a practicum are often listed. Design, production, and use of audiovisual media and micro-computers in libraries were frequent additions.

Some other required courses for students preparing to be youth services librarians in school or public library settings were listed by one or more institutions: planning information systems for children and young adults, oral programming for libraries, public library interagency cooperation, psychology of childhood and adolescence, multicultural librarianship, information transfer and children, communication and learning theory, inner city seminar, and teaching of reading. Most of the electives listed were variations of children's literature—e.g., information books for children, fantasy books for children, folklore and storytelling, multicultural literature for youth, contemporary literature for children, criticism of children's literature, history and development of literature for children, media for minorities, topics in literature for children and young adults (with variation from term to term), puppetry, and bibliotherapy. Another elective of interest was computer coordination for media centers.

One respondent cautioned against too much emphasis on special courses for youth services librarians. Many of the courses in a library school curriculum look at the information needs of youth as part of a larger perspective, she noted. She suggested that a content analysis of all courses offered would be a better way of determining what library schools are offering that youth services librarians need. It is indeed a point well taken although the task is beyond the scope of this survey.

A recent curriculum revision at The University of Michigan was developed by determining the essential content (competencies, skills, knowledge) for all graduate students in the program and then the additional content needed by those in each of the special curriculum plans offered. This planning process resulted in a number of new courses and a restructuring of most remaining ones. The faculty, working together over time on this revision, reaffirmed that, to a considerable extent, information professionals of all kinds have need for common learnings.

We found that several of the special emphases which had made school library media programs different—varied media, the understanding of technology necessary for their use, and even the instructional role of the librarian—have been mainstreamed by the profession. For example, a new course at Michigan, "Design of Information Products," adapted from a course in instructional development which has been taken almost exclusively by students in the school library media concentration, was praised recently as highly desirable for students preparing for their own specializations by academic and public library members of Michigan Dean Robert Warner's advisory committee as well as by representatives from the information industry with whom the school has consulted. In addition, a program component on "communication," long required of school library media specialists, is now required for all students.

Table 2 reports the increase, decrease, and no change in number of courses and faculty, full and part-time, within the past two years, according to those responding to the survey described earlier. Ten institutions (19 percent) have increased the number of courses related to children's and young adult materials and service which they offer. Only one institution has decreased course offerings in this area. Most institutions (thirty-four or 65 percent) report no change, and seven (14 percent) did not respond to this question.

Loss in numbers of full-time faculty within the past two years is reported by five institutions (10 percent). That is higher than the decrease in courses reported and should signal concern. Also, a slightly lower number of institutions reported an increase in full-time faculty within the past two years than the reported increase in courses offered (eight or 15 percent). A large majority of institutions (71 percent or thirty-seven) reported no change within this time period. For part-time faculty, increases were greater (sixteen or 31 percent) within the past two years. Only one institution reported decreased part-time faculty, and twenty-six (50 percent) reported no change.

In reporting plans for program emphasis within the next five years, twenty-two respondents (42 percent) said their institutions plan to increase, two (4 percent) said they expect to decrease emphasis, and twenty-six (50 percent) said they do not expect any change in emphasis. Only two institutions (4 percent) did not respond to this question.

TABLE 2
CHANGES IN GRADUATE PROGRAMS FOR YOUTH SERVICES LIBRARIANS

	Increase		*Decrease*		*No Change*		*No Response*	
	No.	*Per-* *centage*	No.	*Per-* *centage*	No.	*Per-* *centage*	No.	*Per-* *centage*
Number of Courses (past 2 yrs)	10	19	1	2	34	65	7	14
Number of F/T Faculty (past 2 yrs)	8	15	5	10	37	71	2	4
Number of P/T Faculty (past 2 yrs)	16	31	1	2	26	50	9	17
Plans for Emphasis (next 5 yrs)	22	42	2	4	26	50	2	4

N = 52 Institutions

It should be noted that a much larger survey, "School Library Media Employment Questionnaire," was distributed to institutions with programs preparing school library media specialists by the American Association for School Librarian's Library Media Educators Section. Results from this survey should be of considerable interest to the field. That questionnaire did not seek information about public library youth services placement and projected need, however.

Of the fifty-two institutions represented in the present survey, forty (77 percent) reported that they had offered one or more continuing education (CE) programs intended for school and/or public library youth services librarians during the past two years. The range for all institutions was zero to seventeen within this time period. Table 3 shows the number of institutions which offered any of the following types of CE programs: (1) those given for academic credit and therefore applicable for a graduate degree, (2) those given for continuing education units (CEUs) as approved by the institution or by a state agency established to coordinate continuing education, and (3) those given as noncredit workshops, conferences, or seminars. Three library schools offered six or more continuing education courses for academic credit, another five institutions offered three to five CE programs for academic credit, and seventeen offered one or two such programs during the past two years. Twenty-five institutions, slightly less than half of the total response group of fifty-two, reported offering continuing education programs for academic credit to youth services librarians.

Programs offering CEU credits were not given quite as often for this audience. Two institutions gave six or more programs, six gave three to five programs, and fourteen gave one or two programs. The total number of institutions offering programs directed to youth services librarians for CEUs was twenty-two.

Noncredit programs for this audience were given by still fewer institutions; none gave six or more programs without credit, six gave three to five programs, and twelve gave one or two during the past two years. Although

TABLE 3
CONTINUING EDUCATION FOR YOUTH SERVICES LIBRARIANS
WITHIN THE PAST TWO YEARS

Type of Program	*Number of Programs*				
	6 or more	*3-5*	*1-2*	*0*	*No Response*
Academic Credit	3	5	17	4	23
CEUs	2	6	14	3	27
Noncredit	0	6	12	3	31

Number of Institutions offering 1 or more CE Programs in the past two years = 40 (77 percent)
Range of CE Programs offered = 0-17

the total number of institutions giving this type of continuing education program is smaller than the number giving either of the credit type programs (eighteen), the noncredit activities described by respondents seem to attract larger numbers of participants, often 200 or more for a single event. Thus they do provide a useful function in the professional development of youth services librarians. This may be especially important in geographic areas where other agencies—professional associations, regional service units, or interagency consortia—are not providing such a function. But even if other groups are available, there is value for the library school and for the practitioner to interact on matters of updating professional knowledge.

An impressive and extensive list of CE topics for credit and noncredit was offered by those responding to the questionnaire. They included many facets of materials and services of interest to youth services librarians. Several library schools offer updates on different topics for this audience each year. Some are day long activities, others are one week mini-courses, and still others are offered via television or on a series of Saturdays. It seems safe to say that most library schools would respond positively to almost any suggestion for continuing education activities they received from youth services practitioners.

Responses were mixed to the question: Within the past two years, to what extent have practitioners who work with youth participated in your continuing education activities which were *not* designed especially for this group (e.g., searching automated databases, financial management for librarians, using microcomputers in libraries)? Some respondents said they had no statistics to reflect the degree of participation of any type of professional in their continuing education activities, and others indicated little participation in these general interest topics. One respondent interpreted the question as meaning a lack of importance in these topics for school or public librarians who work with children or young adults. This was certainly not intended. A fair number of library schools reported experiences similar to those at Michigan in which a growing number of youth services librarians are seeking the same kind of professional development as are their colleagues in adult services in academic, special, and public libraries. Particularly in the areas noted earlier—online searching, management skills, and microcomputer applications—information professionals of many specialties seem to be feeling the need for more experience and acting on that need to gain or renew skills.

Conclusions

In summarizing the findings of this survey and drawing conclusions from it, I am modestly optimistic about what library schools are offering youth services practitioners and those who wish careers in this arena. A large majority of library schools are offering graduate programs with curriculum plans in one or both of the youth services library settings, school or public. All but two of the institutions from which responses were received report that they have one or more faculty members in this area; for forty-nine (94 percent) of the total responding group of fifty-two, at least one of these faculty members has full-time status. This means that someone is there to listen to the needs of youth services librarians and to speak to those needs in curriculum planning activities of the institution.

The percent of graduates who have taken youth services positions in the past two years varies from one institution to another; for the majority in this survey, one-fourth or more of the total number of graduates took such a position. But many institutions, as is true with the library school at Michigan, would welcome the opportunity to increase the number. Twenty-two library schools reported that they plan greater emphasis for this specialization within the next five years. Several are actively recruiting students now to meet the need for youth services professionals in both school and public libraries. These and other library schools may find valuable support for such an action from this Allerton Conference and from the AASL survey mentioned earlier. Few institutions reported decreases in number of courses within the past two years.

The most negative indicator is that five institutions (10 percent) have decreased the number of full-time faculty who have teaching responsibility and expertise in materials and library services for youth. It is hoped and believed that this figure will be reversed in the next two to five years.

Continuing education to meet the needs of youth services practitioners appears to be healthy; many types of programs are offered and most library schools participate in some CE activities for this audience. Not all relevant CE is, or should be, directed exclusively to this audience. If youth services librarians are a part of the mainstream of the information profession, as they must be, then all instructors must understand and courses throughout the curriculum must address the needs of this group within the context of the total professional education as well as through separate segments of that educational program.

JUDITH A. DRESCHER

Director of Libraries
Memphis/Shelby County Public Library and Information Center
Memphis, Tennessee

What Do Public Libraries Need From Managers and Missionaries for Children's Services?

As a former children's services librarian and a library administrator in several public libraries, I've spoken on this topic numerous times over the last twelve years. In general, the audience expects to hear words of wisdom about how children's librarians need to know the literature in the field and the wide range of needs of their varied audiences, how to budget, how to select materials and do programming, and how to get the administrator's attention. Certainly an M.L.S., a little experience in the field, and some continuing education will provide an awareness of these needs. Therefore, it is obvious that libraries and children's services librarians can address needs other than those that are specific to children's librarianship.

Over the years many librarians have realized that those in children's services need to know more than just the literature of the field. For instance, only after I ceased being a children's librarian did I have a conversation with a friend who explained the development of motor skills in young children. With chagrin, I realized that almost all the finger plays selected for use in programming had been inappropriate and probably very frustrating.

Children's services librarians need to know about child development (both mental and physical) as well as how children learn to read. Although not all practitioners agree with the methods used in schools, we need to know the current methods being used in our schools and, more importantly, we need to be aware of curriculum changes. Just as we need to know about child development, we need to know how children build vocabulary skills, word recognition, sentence patterns, and comprehension.

Most children's services librarians, even in very large systems, do their own public relations so they need to know what sells their programs and how to put it into a format that will "talk" to children or those who pay

137

attention to library services for children. Program planning is a necessity for all children's librarians and one that takes great skill. Children's services librarians would do well to spend time learning how to put together a good program as well as concentrating on the content.

But, I'd like to move on to a larger issue. After the basics are there, what do libraries need from children's librarians? I would suggest the following: advocacy, political savvy, initiative, commitment, pride, and professionalism.

Although Frances Clark Sayers (1965) is most often quoted for her insightful comments on the philosophy of librarianship to children, I particularly like her quote from *Summoned by Books* when she says: "If she (the children's librarian) is left outside the realm of the intellectual and administrative concern of the library staff with which she works, she had better look to her own attitudes" (p. 44).

As a library administrator, I market and sell library services everyday. I also react to "being sold" a service or library product that I am convinced will benefit both the public and position the library in a prominent and respected place in the community. Without well planned, specific advocacy on the part of children's librarians, the library administration will respond to its own agenda or to those on the staff who are pushing certain services. Children's services librarians have consistently suffered from the syndrome of waiting for the recognition they know they deserve and it's obvious that that isn't working.

Closely aligned with advocacy is political savvy. In other words, what is going on in your community that is such an obvious match with service to children that you could use it to make children's services a higher priority in your library? Learn to translate local community efforts, interests, and plans into needs for library service. Watch for issues that surface in every community—emphasis on job training, education, community education centers, preschoolers, reading readiness—and make certain that the library is involved. Make a plan, call whoever is in charge, tell them what you can do for them. Learn to think of the library as a place that can offer infinite possibilities for services and translate those possibilities for others in the community who don't think of the library that way.

Libraries are always looking for employees with initiative, but it is believed that children's librarians need initiative more than others. You are often the only professional who exclusively serves children in your library (a lonely spot) so it takes more and harder efforts to do the work that needs to be done and be the standard bearer for children's services. Make certain that initiative is recognized by volunteering to give reports to friends groups and the library board about what is happening in children's services and why. Parlay your ability and initiative into becoming recognized as a valuable and respected voice for children's services.

Commitment and pride are two needs that go closely together. I have made it a point to always tell others about my beginnings in the profession, and I have advocated and supported children's service as an administrator. Too often, however, I have watched children's services librarians negate their own image by both downgrading what they do and permitting others to do it. Students often ask me where I learned to be a library director and I always tell them I learned two excellent skills as a children's librarian— how to tell a story and how to manage a crowd of three-year olds! Children's services librarians need to decide that they are going to commit themselves to being a good one and make certain others know how good they are.

Libraries need librarians who look, act, and perform in a professional manner. We can learn much from professionals in other fields when we recognize that they are consciously portraying an image to the public that *they* want the public to believe. Be very aware that you are always representing the library profession and the institution for which you work—if you don't like the image, you are in control of changing it.

Finally, I know what to look for in children's services librarians. I want to know that you decided to become one, that you know what you're doing, but, more importantly, *why* you're doing it, that you have the ability to articulate that why to varied audiences (including me), that you can see the possibilities of library service to children in everything that happens around you, and be able to determine how and why some of them fit into library service. I look for the philosopher, the dreamer, the innovator who is part pragmatic realist. Coupled with practical library skills, this is what public libraries are searching for in their children's services librarians.

NOTE

Sayers, F. C. (1965). *Summoned by books, essays and speeches by Frances Clarke Sayers.* New York: Viking.

DELORES ZACHARY PRETLOW

Supervisor of Media Services
Richmond Public Schools
Richmond, Virginia

What Do Schools Need?

After eighteen years of professional commitment to library media services for youth, I found myself perplexed by the question, What do schools need? Perplexed because my personal perceptions were so clear—or so I thought. Yet, I could not focus and translate them to the written word. It became necessary to sit and recall years of professional behaviors and experiences in the school and public library. It also became necessary to summon relationships and accomplishments, gained or lost, due to those behaviors.

What I saw showed growth and tremendous change, but not nearly enough. It was frightening because I found that the majority of our problems were due to us; we did not know who we were or what we should be doing. I turned to research and fellow professionals for help. I had to know what was being done in the school library media centers of this country. There was too much fragmentation in my mind and in the evidence to determine what was needed now and tomorrow. What I discerned schools to need from librarianship and what I see them needing in the future was tied to how we perceived ourselves as being and what role we are willing to play.

Visualize this scenario. The school doors open at least thirty minutes before the morning bell. The children begin to enter—slowly, sleepily, but with a destination in mind. The library media center is warm, cozy, and there is a person there frantically trying to get ready for the day. Some books that really need to be processed came in late yesterday. A teacher is waiting for them. There are still four unusable media kits from last week, returned with parts missing. An order needs to go out for replacement of the parts. A class is coming in at first period and the schedule shows that classes will continue until fifth period. Lunchtime work is out of the question—cafeteria duty. There is a faculty meeting this afternoon so no after school catch-up. The curriculum team is meeting, and the busy library media specialist really wants to prepare some bibliographies for the units to be studied next, even though not invited to do so. Two projectors

141

need to be moved from their security location to classrooms for first period, and they need to be checked before going out.

The faces appear in the door and see the distressed expression of the library media specialist. Some just want to view magazines, some have reports due, and some are looking for a book that a friend returned. If you were one of the students, would you ask the library media specialist for anything? If you were the library media specialist, would you *want* the students to ask?

James Liesner (1984) in "Learning at Risk: School Library Media Programs in an Information World" states a premise school library media specialists should contemplate:

> Considerable confusion exists regarding the roles library media specialists do or do not perform and the roles they are capable of performing. Roles cannot be performed and services cannot be used effectively if they are not perceived accurately by potential clients or if there is a lack of acceptance of these roles by either the individuals receiving the benefits of them, or the individuals attempting to perform them. Role conflicts of this sort almost inevitably lead to job dissatisfaction and ineffective performance. (p. 76)

"Capable of performing" is one significant phrase of this excerpt. Most school library media specialists have educational backgrounds. They have been trained as teachers and, therefore, curriculum theory and instructional design are part of the expertise brought to the field of library media. Skills instruction—which by default, lack of acceptance, or ignorance—is often taught in isolation. Library media specialists are not, as a whole, invited or even considered to be a part of the school curriculum team.

This brings up another issue in Liesner's excerpt which is "roles cannot be performed accurately by potential clients or if there is a lack of acceptance of these roles by either the individuals receiving the benefits of them or the individuals attempting to perform them." Although the library media center has been called the "hub" of the school, the actuality of this occurring is not universal.

The role designation of the specialists is not seen as a support position. Olson (1984) in "Unassailable Truth? A Look at the Concept of School Library Media Specialists as Teachers," cites "the problem is that we have been too literal in our interpretation and demonstration attempts at curriculum support....such support should be far more direct. In fact...the library is a *part* of the curriculum" (p. 55). He submits that we must stop thinking about the library as a resource, a service, and start thinking about it as a subject, a course requiring direct instruction to achieve its objectives" (p. 56).

The need is evident for library media specialists to accept themselves and to determine their "place" in the scheme of educating children. Inherent in this acceptance is the need to educate teachers and administrators, not just of the importance of the school media program, but, more significantly, the role the library media specialist plays in the accomplishment of the total program. Only with this sense of being needed and expected to perform can both the school and the library media specialist attain the desired results.

In order for job satisfaction to be a basic part of the work life of the library media specialist, evidence of self-confident professionalism is necessary, even if forced. This self-confident professionalism is shown when library media specialists come out of the center office performing clerical tasks only and enter the mainstream of the school's instructional program.

Hambleton (1982) offers another response to role designation as seen through an analysis of studies on school library media specialists and programs by various school-based individuals as well as by media specialists themselves.

> In the numerous studies carried out in the past twenty years, a number of conclusions are common: that the school librarian's perception of that role differs significantly from that of others in the educational system, that the school library seems to play only a marginal role in the total educational program, and that the low regard for the school librarian militates against a direct involvement in the instructional program of the school. (pp. 18-20)

The impact of the perceived role designation, or lack thereof, of the library media specialist was further cited by Judy Pitts (1984) in "A Creative Survey of Research Concerning Role Expectations of Library Media Specialists." Four of these findings are summarized below:

1. Today's library media specialists preferred the traditional services of acquisition and distribution, as opposed to instructional development, evaluation, and utilization.
2. Professional media specialists could communicate to teachers the instruction role they played much better than part-time or nonprofessional library media specialists.
3. Librarians with more diversified interests exhibited more involvement in the curriculum.
4. Librarians with low self-images spent more of their work time in the media center doing clerical tasks and less work with students (pp. 164-69).

These findings, coupled with the research excerpt of Hambleton, create the frame of mind necessary to eliminate the negative aspects of what we need to be to and for schools and promote planning for the future. Understanding this research may be just the impetus for library media specialists to become more aggressive in their discipline. We must be aggressive in order to promote the field and its necessity, not merely relevance, to the educational arena by showing the achievements and benefits to young people. "School library media specialists and children's librarians have long had specialized programs to meet special needs; then some degree of specialization in other areas became the rule" (Hannigan, 1984, p. 24). The specialization, more than likely, has been in a content area, or in general elementary education/teaching.

Just as we promote freedom to read, we have promoted putting mechanisms into place to allow personal participation in what children read and view outside the library media center walls. "Technological advancements have redefined the role of the school media specialist in the 1980's from that of a collector of resources and administrator of a facility to that of a teacher and instructional designer" (Hortin, 1985, pp. 20-21).

Reading any of the literature enhances the knowledge that school media specialists, along with being teachers and instructional designers, are setting priorities as participants in the instructional program. We are bringing to the table personal expertise in research skills, teaching methodology, curriculum development, etc. We are integrating the standards of learning and collection development into the overall pattern of classroom instruction, which is as it should be. Consequently, the role of the library media specialist becomes a more integral part of, and reinforces the role of, the classroom teacher.

Liesner states that it is time to accept and develop the information intermediary function that we perform and not worry about whether we are teachers or not. Of course we perform a teaching function, but it should be based on our own discipline and related to the essential intermediary role we are playing and need to expand and improve (Liesner, 1984, p. 85). No longer do we need to carry the self-imposed weight of feeling like second-class teachers or of considering ourselves as "enrichment for the basics rather than as the fodder on which learning can thrive; enrichment, like butter on bread, can be scraped off or done without when times get tough" (Loertscher, 1982, pp. 415-21). Loertscher goes on to say: "If library media specialists can take the best programming ideas they have now and integrate them into the instructional program...they will be demonstrating their worth instead of just talking about it" (p. 421).

This, then, is what we need to be to schools. The library media specialists, moving toward expansion of services to meet the intellectual needs of a more technologically advanced society, demanding higher level skills, and more complex means of integrating those skills into a multifaceted curriculum design is, indeed, what we should be accomplishing.

It is universally understood that "the keeper of the books" is now the "information keeper/retriever/disseminator." "The older concepts of passive culture repositories or centers for the development of an enjoyment and appreciation for reading good books while identifying very important functions, do not appear to be actively responsive to the entire range of needs identified as crucial for survival and achievement in an extremely complex, information and rapidly changing world" (Liesner, 1984, p. 69). What are school library media specialists doing to secure their effectiveness in the twenty-first century? It is safe to say that if we are professionally astute, we are:

1. soliciting the support of school administrators;
2. sponsoring and presenting in-service programs for the teachers with whom we work;
3. producing much needed instructional materials not available through commercial sources or too expensive to purchase;
4. managing media centers with computer programs designed to provide the much needed time for student and teacher joint efforts;
5. training students to use the electronic formats of information retrieval so that a broader base of research is at their fingertips;
6. accepting responsibility for and asking to be part of contributing to the curriculum design effort of the school program;
7. providing, for preview purposes, newly produced/printed materials in an effort to bring teachers and administrators into the selection process; in this manner they gain a commitment to and a responsibility for the importance of collection development based on the educational philosophy of the program;
8. acknowledging that we may be our own worst enemies in not actively seeking and establishing our role in the total scheme of educating children;
9. sharing with each other goals and dreams for what can be done and what has been done, and, in so doing, learning from, with, and for each other;
10. adamantly stating personnel worth and justifiably taking credit for accomplishments;
11. developing curricula of library skills to be integrated into the subject content areas; thus showing the significant impact of the field on all others, and broadening the scope of educating youth, and;
12. reaching out to other libraries and agencies to supplement needed materials, gain additional support, and make them active participants in the goal and knowledgeability of the role of the library media specialist.

If the twenty-first century is to look bright, library media specialists must become not only accountable, but accomplished in their role and with the impact of it on the education of youth. The confusion over role designation has not kept library media specialists from moving forward. What we should be doing is evidenced by the apparent knowledge and understanding of what we have been doing, the desire to determine what the schools need, and the determination to reach that need, mitigate the negative effects of what has not been done and cause us to move forward.

NOTES

Hambleton, A. (1982, May/June). Static in the educational intercom: Conflict and school librarian. *Emergency Librarian, 9,* 18.

Hannigan, J. (1984). Vision to purpose to power: A quest for excellence in the education of library and information science professionals. In *Libraries and the learning society: Papers in response to a nation at risk* (p. 24). Chicago: American Library Association.

Hortin, J. A. (1985, September). The changing role of the school media specialist. *Tech Trends, 36,* 20-21.

Liesner, J. W. (1984). Learning at risk: School library media programs in an information world. In *Libraries and the learning society: Papers in response to a nation at risk.* Chicago: American Library Association.

Loertscher, D. (1982a, February). School library media centers: The revolutionary past. *Wilson Library Bulletin, 56,* 416.

Loertscher, D. (1982b, February). The second revolution: A taxonomy for the 1980s. *Wilson Library Bulletin, 56,* 421.

Olson, L. W. (1984, Fall). Unassailable truth? A look at the concept of school library media specialists as teachers. *School Library Media Quarterly, 12,* 55.

Pitts, J. M. (1982, Winter). A creative survey of research concerning role expectations of library media specialists. *School Library Media Quarterly, 10,* 164-169.

GERALD G. HODGES

School of Library and Information Science
University of Iowa
Iowa City, Iowa

Evaluation and Measurement of Youth Services

The current effort to improve the quality of youth services and to expand these services must be firmly grounded in a meaningful context of evaluation. Evaluation of personnel and measurement and evaluation of program are essential components of any program which is striving for excellence in the delivery of needed services. Every time personnel evaluation is considered, I am reminded of the principal at my first position as a school library media specialist.

He felt that the best methods of evaluating my performance (and, truthfully, my program by extension) was to count the frequency with which I changed the bulletin boards in the library. I suppose you could develop some output measure for this. It was very soon found that students were more adept at this, and soon another measure of performance (and of my program) became the number of students who were involved in library media center activities. The true problem encountered here was that my job description really only evolved—there was never sufficient prior planning between me and the principal for what I intended to accomplish. And this prior planning does appear to be one of the most important components of developing meaningful methods for program and personnel evaluation. If this does not occur, there is the real problem in schools of library media specialists being evaluated on the same basis as classroom teachers, a process which does not fully address all the activities of library media specialists, regardless of how much we teach.

Youth services librarians, regardless of their institution, should have a major voice in communicating to their superiors the types of desired evaluation processes and methods. This input can help administrators see very clearly the relationship of library services in a school to the instructional program or the roles which children's and young adult librarians are playing in achieving the public library's goals.

A process of communication in which goals are determined, in which priorities among library functions are established, and in which performance measures (or quality indicators) are defined is essential. There is a real need for youth librarians to be evaluated in terms of their jobs and not on the basis of some particular conception of librarianship which may have little relationship to the actual job at hand. If performance is not going to be evaluated by your planning with teachers, there will likely be little payoff for spending the time, energy, and intelligence which that entails. On the other hand, if you minimize in advance the importance of the clerical and technical aspects of your program, then this conception of librarianship will not play as important a part in performance evaluation. So then, performance evaluation measures should be planned in advance, should be job specific, should be viewed positively, should be ongoing in the sense that they can be modified as program goals are modified, and should provide some indicators and measures for assessing the extent to which the librarian is meeting or exceeding expectations.

The process of performance evaluation should be based upon the most appropriate mix of methods for a given situation. Each librarian should work to make certain that the best data can be gathered to determine effectiveness and to indicate areas for improvement and growth. Methods which might be considered in determining the most appropriate mix are: establishing performance standards or competencies; establishing specific levels of acceptable performance on these criteria; supervisor observation of performance (here it is extremely important that a conference be held prior to the observation so that the supervisor will understand the purposes of the activities); supervisor review of performance; peer and client review of performance (in a school setting, important data for performance improvement can be gained by systematically gaining input from teachers and students); systematic self-assessment (it truly is renewing to have the opportunity to examine the extent to which personal and professional goals are being attained); and objective assessment of the degree of attainment of institutional goals.

Those in youth librarianship have available a multitude of instruments which recently have been developed to evaluate the performance of youth librarians. These can be of great assistance in the development of instruments for local use. A clever idea is to make adaptations of existing instruments since evaluation in the best sense is a local process to meet local goals.

Goal Setting for Youth Library Programs

One of the clearest ways for youth library services to be more visible and to communicate program excellence is through the intricate and necessary process of the establishment of program goals. Without the direction of goals, it is difficult, if not impossible, to evaluate programs in meaningful ways. In schools, the interactive process of working with students, faculty, and administrators helps ensure that library program goals are derived from school goals and that the program functions which flow from these goals are consistent with the curricular and instructional objectives of the school. A major benefit of this interactive involvement is that many schools report that library and information skills goals have become a part of the stated goals and priorities for the school.

In public libraries there are numerous methods for the establishment of goals for youth services which are congruent with the goals of the parent institution. The *Planning Process for Public Libraries* enables an individual institution to determine those goals and consequently the objectives which will give direction to library programs and to budget allocations. We need to begin to gather data on a national basis which will communicate the importance of youth services within libraries. Many public libraries, both voluntarily and as requirements for accreditation, are collecting and reporting output measures. There is considerable anecdotal evidence that youth services may account for large portions of the circulation per capita, turnover rate, attendance per capita, and registration per capita of the library's output measures. We should make a concerted effort in each library to determine the proportion which youth services contribute as a justification on the local level for staff, budgets, etc., and to make youth services even more visible to library staff and trustees. In the effort to help each child in the United States receive a public library card by the end of 1987, we can certainly see youth services expanding across the nation. Now is probably exactly the time to begin to measure and report our effectiveness and accomplishments. A joint effort among the youth divisions (YASD, AASL, and ALSC) of ALA should be undertaken to assist local libraries in gathering and reporting data regarding the current status of youth services.

In all libraries serving youth, a critical part of the evaluation process is to use measures which will gauge the satisfaction of users, actual and potential, with services and collections. An analysis of demographic data will indicate who our clients are. Measures need to be developed which will help determine penetration, or the use of the services by the user population; availability (why an available service is not being used or to determine why an unavailable desired service is not being made available); and determine the degree of satisfaction with the services of both users and staff.

Some cringe at the thought of measurement and reporting of services, feeling that some currently available measures are too primitive, mechanistic, or rudimentary to come close to conveying the quality of the human interactions in library services. Some librarians say that they simply do not have the time to collect data in order to report measures of effectiveness. We appear, however, to be in an era when the gathering and reporting of data is so essential to the continued improvement of youth services that we simply must make time and make certain that the measures used do have meaning for us.

As indicated earlier, we have the responsibility for determining the goals and measures which are appropriate for our library. This also gives us the responsibility for measuring the extent to which those goals have been achieved or exceeded. When budget crunches come, we should not have to rely on the good graces of funding authorities, hoping that they nostalgically will remember children's services. It has become clear that in many school systems library services are among the first to be considered for cutbacks. We must now be prepared for interpreting and justifying current levels of funding and services and also be prepared for having realistic plans for program expansion. An essential element of this process is the identification of the audience to be served. The youth divisions of ALA have the opportunity and need to define by age who is a child, an early adolescent, and a young adult. In order to present, on a national level, a status report of youth services, we need to be able to define terms. If we do not, there will be scant comparability of data and the prospects are that youth services may suffer.

Measurement of Services—Some New Possibilities

The use of output measures has indeed become widely accepted in public libraries, and school library media specialists should develop measures which are meaningful for reporting progress in the library media program. The available output measures, as noted earlier, do not address some of the important elements of our programs, elements which merit more sophisticated methods of measurement. The extent to which the school library media specialist performs the instructional role, engages in the provision of access to students and collection evaluation, and the extent of promotion of materials through reading guidance are four areas which will serve as illustrations of where new measurement methods might be utilized.

Instructional Role Quotient

In school library media programs, we must demonstrate a high level of involvement in the instructional programs of schools. There is a real need to demonstrate to ourselves and to administrators that we are making the best possible uses of the collections and of our competence in instructional development. The personalization of instruction implies very strongly a systematic approach to the decisions regarding the best learning alternatives for each student. In the past we have typically relied on reporting numbers of teachers with whom we have teamed, numbers of classes which have used the media center's collection, and percentages of students taught. These appear to be rudimentary in that we are penalized for that teacher who simply will not use materials other than a textbook and a chalkboard, and these measures do not allow for the varying amount of time involved in various levels of working with teachers. I have developed an Instructional Role Quotient which might help present a more accurate and more positive picture of what we are doing when working in this capacity. Also, after gathering baseline data, a quotient such as this might be used in establishing goals for improvement (see Figure 1).

$$IRQ = \frac{6a + 4b + 2c + d - e}{n}$$

a = planning, implementing, and evaluating instruction with teacher(s); teaching library media skills when appropriate; certainly correlating library media center materials with instructional objectives; may or may not include grading of student work; may or may not include local production of materials; may or may not include gathering resources from other information agencies; does include evaluating the effectiveness of the materials used.

b = provision of materials to meet instructional objectives after planning session(s) with teachers(s); faculty involvement in selection of titles for these objectives will count here. No evaluation of effectiveness of materials.

c = Provide guidance to students who come from a class requiring information, without planning with teacher(s).

d = Acquire and organize materials in the subject area.

e = Instructional materials are not available to support the unit.

n = Number of applicable units in the designated time period (NOTE: the time period is your decision; suggestions are a full year, semester, or grading period).

Figure 1. Instructional Role Quotient (IRQ)

This formula will give credit for the amount of work involved in planning with teachers and will not overly penalize for the teachers who do not use media center materials, even when the units are applicable. An example of the use of this formula follows:

$$IRQ = \frac{6a + 4b + 2c + d - e}{n}$$

$$IRQ = \frac{6(2) + 4(12) + 2(60) + 19 - 1 = 198}{80 \qquad\qquad 80}$$

$$IRQ = 2.475$$

In the earlier example, there are eighty applicable units during the designated time period (n). In two (a) of the units, you work with the teacher in planning, implementing, and evaluating instruction. In twelve (b) you correlate materials with the objectives; in sixty (c) you work with students who need information; in nineteen (d) materials are available; and in one (e) there are no materials available. In this example, the IRQ is 2.475 on a scale of 6.000 to negative 1.000. Your goal then may be to maintain an IRQ of 2.475 or increase this quotient to a higher number.

Access Quotients

Many libraries report attendance figures, either average daily attendance or visits per capita, or other. These statistics do not reflect the purposes of use. Padding attendance figures with students who are simply attending a study hall and not using materials or using the library as a dating center are not the best ways of communicating access. "Purposes of use" is a concept which we must help administrators (and users) consider as priorities. The following Daily Access Quotient (DAQ) helps shed light on the activities which users pursue in our centers (see Figure 2).

In the twenty-day period (n), note that 950 students attended the media center, and the average daily attendance was 47.500. The earlier mentioned DAQ is best used for in-house measurement of use since it is influenced by the number of students in the school and other internal factors. A standardized figure would be to consider enrollment and could be presented as the per capita access quotient (PCAQ).

$$PCAQ = \frac{4x + 4y + 3z + a - sh}{s}$$

s = number of students

$$PCAQ = \frac{2750}{500}$$

$$PCAQ = 5.500$$

$$DAQ = \frac{4x + 4y + 3z + a - sh}{n}$$

x = number of students you teach library-related content, either inside or outside the media center.

y = number of students working on activities and with materials you have planned for specific instructional objectives (generally this would be in periods following instruction or introduction).

z = number of students working independently in using library media center materials;

a = number of students attending with no discernible purpose;

sh = number of students assigned to the library media center for study hall;

n = number of days.

EXAMPLE:

$$DAQ = \frac{4x + 4y + 3z + a - sh}{n}$$

$$DAQ = \frac{4(200) + 4(200) + 3(300) + 250 - 0 = 2750}{2020}$$

$$DAQ = 137.500$$

Figure 2. Daily Access Quotient (DAQ)

Collection Evaluation Measures

In measurement and justification of library services, we often focus exclusively on inputs (e.g., twelve books/student) and have not done enough in measuring the effectiveness of collections. This becomes especially critical when proposing additional expenditures for materials. Using a clever combination of input and output measures can paint a clearer picture for funding bodies of how much "bang for the buck" we are getting from our rather high-cost collections.

David Loertscher has developed methods for collection "mapping" of general and specialized collections in terms of instructional objectives.

This is a means of telling us where the collections are strong and where they need more titles to meet adequately the instructional needs of students. School districts should use this mapping approach to determine the most appropriate statistics for determining exemplary collections as opposed to those making progress. Local assessment is essential here.

Public and school libraries should both be gathering data regarding in-house use of all collections. This is particularly important for reference collections, periodicals, vertical files, and other collections whose use is not reflected in circulation statistics. This is also particularly important for libraries serving the information needs of young adults.

In justifying any monies for materials, but most importantly for those high-cost items such as reference works, we should provide data regarding the cost per use. For example, if an encyclopedia set costs $500, some may feel that the old outdated set will last another year. However, if it is known that each set receives approximately 2,000 uses per year, then the cost per use is only 25 cents. A means of justifying periodical subscriptions is also cost per use. If a periodical costs $20 and the total uses of current and back issues is 200 in a year, then the cost per use of that periodical for that year is 10 cents. These figures should be readily available both for in-house and external reporting.

It is also becoming increasingly important to consider the concept of document delivery rate or "lag time" in providing information sources for children and young adults. Baseline data should be gathered and questions should be posed regarding the acceptability of the lag time and decisions made regarding steps to take to reduce this figure.

Reading Guidance Quotient

A function dear to all of us is providing guidance to users of the collections. An in-house measure to determine how well materials are promoted can be expressed as a Reading Guidance Quotient (see Figure 3).

In this example, fifty new titles were promoted using direct, specially designed direct and indirect methods for each title. No title went straight to the shelves. The range in this formula is 6.000 to negative 1.000.

The purpose of this presentation has been to reinforce the theme of the conference—managers and missionaries. I believe that youth services librarians are missionaries in the best definition of that term. If we can bolster fervor with measurement and evaluation data which justify our great faith and zeal, then we as managers of change can hopefully achieve the type of future sought for youth services. Cooperative efforts among the youth divisions of ALA, among library school educators, and among all librarians serving youth, regardless of type of library, can help us as a unified coalition bring about the scenarios established at this landmark conference.

$$RGQ = \frac{3d + 2sdi + id - sos}{n}$$

d = number of titles promoted by DIRECT reading
reading guidance techniques; e.g., booktalking,
book discussion, individual referral (either
oral or written), reviews in newspapers, cable
TV exposure, etc.

sdi = number of titles promoted by SPECIALLY DESIGNED
INDIRECT techniques; e.g., pathfinders, "What to Read
After You Read...," thematic bookmarks;
thematic displays, etc.

id = number of titles promoted by other INDIRECT
techniques—e.g., display books, general
listing of new arrivals, etc.

sos = number of titles with no promotion
(straight on shelves)

n = number of possible titles (this will vary;
you may be promoting one portion of the
collection, or new arrivals, or...).

EXAMPLE:

$$RGQ = \frac{3d + 2sdi + id - sos}{n}$$

$$RGQ = \frac{3(50) + 2(50) + 50 - 0 = 300}{50 \qquad 50}$$

$RGQ = 6.000$

Figure 3. Reading Guidance Quotient (RGQ)

DAWN H. HELLER

Media Services Coordinator
Riverside-Brookfield High School
Riverside, Illinois

Developing a Youth Agenda
for the Information Age

Looking at this audience of some 200 professionals dedicated to improving library services to children and young adults, I am reminded of a story about Don Adcock's daughter. Some of you know Don—director of Library Services for the Glen Ellyn, Illinois elementary school district, and active in state and national library associations.

Some years ago he told me that one of his daughters in the early elementary grades was asked as a class assignment to draw a picture of what her mother or father did as "their job." She drew her dad driving a car. During the "show and tell" phase of this occupation study unit, she explained her father's occupation. He wasn't a taxi driver nor a traveling salesman. She explained that her dad was a librarian—he went to meetings. There is a postscript to this story. Don's daughter is now an adult and is now the director of a public library in a small town in Illinois, and now she goes to meetings too.

We all have ways of rating these library-related meetings. In addition to perceptions of the quality of programming and vitality of participants, we often have a subjective yardstick or measure.

As a "Notable Quotable" collector, I am a collector of memorable phrases, apt euphemisms, and vivid images offered by speakers at conferences and institutes. Let me share some of these quotes that I have gathered at this Allerton Institute. (Incidentally, on the basis of both quantity and quality of "Notable Quotables," this has to rate as a Four-Star Meeting.) Perhaps, too, the process will help relive the memorable moments we have shared, and perhaps even help focus on the task of this conference.

Regina Minudri reminded us that: "Most important people have been young adults at some time in their lives!" She also urged us to remember that "while we are speaking on issues, hopefully if not all in one voice, at least in the same key." Let's remember this as work is done on our agenda-building task this morning.

And so we are about to embark on the agenda-building process. It's time to work together to create a document to serve as a plan, a road map for the future using our higher order thinking skills. If we do our work well today, we truly do have the opportunity to fulfill Marilyn Miller's prophesy: "This Allerton will be viewed as a milestone in the development of library service to youth."

The following are the recommendations of the participants of the 1986 Allerton Institute for the Youth Agenda. They are presented by each of the three focus areas examined at the institute.

FOCUS 1
MANAGEMENT OF YOUTH SERVICES:
POLITICAL, FINANCIAL, AND SOCIAL IMPLICATIONS

Recruitment of Youth Services Library Staff on Professional and Paraprofessional Levels

1. Improve the image of youth services workers.
2. Attain pay equity within the profession.
3. Recruit in undergrad programs, schools of education, and from beginning students in library science programs.
4. Establish mentorship programs and other formal contacts between practitioners and students in library school.
5. Define skills and qualities needed for youth services staff.
6. Examine seniority issues in both school and public library settings so that transferring from within the profession is easier.

Coalition-Building

1. ALA youth divisions should work jointly to influence ALA legislation policy where youth issues are involved.
2. ALA youth divisions should train youth librarians to be effective politically and to build coalitions.
3. Professional relationships should be established at the local, state, and national levels both within and outside the profession. Individual librarians, state and regional associations, agencies, and the youth divisions of ALA should be active in coalition-building.
4. Identify and publicize liaisons already existing between youth divisions and other youth-serving associations and organizations, and identify and publicize special projects which show that cooperation works in improving library service for youth.

5. Respect differences between youth services librarians and divisions at all levels and make commitment to working together.
6. Have ALA develop policy and guidelines on coalition-building.
7. Build active liaisons with associations such as professional education associations.

Legislation

1. Develop a proactive stand in supporting legislation for youth.
2. Require state ALA chapters to report annually on legislation to the ALA council pertaining to all types of libraries.

Literacy

1. Identify illiterates including levels of illiteracy and examine motivations to become literate.
2. At the national level, develop a program that provides definition, an awareness campaign, funding for programs for the various target groups, the establishment of a program clearinghouse, and coalition-building.
3. At the state level, provide funding for literacy programs, legislative support, training for library workers, and consultant support.
4. At the local level, provide funding, implement programs, work with other community agencies concerned with literacy, and provide staff and other support to new readers.

Demographics

1. Identify changes in composition of the library community, for example the number of mothers in the work force, information on the current immigrant population, and the growth/reduction of specific age groups, etc.
2. Devise tools for collecting demographic data.
3. Actual collection of data on the local level with data compiled at the state and regional level.
4. Evaluate present services/resources in light of population changes—at the local level.
5. Library education institutions need to recognize changes and adjust curriculum and recruitment strategies.

Librarian as Agent of Change

1. Youth services librarians should be involved in the management and development of library service in the larger sense at the local, state, and national levels.

2. Practitioner and library educators should work together to change and amend library school curricula as needed.

Access to Information for Youth

1. Dissemination of and support of the Library Bill of Rights and Access Statement for School Librarians.
2. Removal of regulations denying access to materials of all forms and formats by age.
3. Education of parents/community on the importance of open access to materials and information for youth.
4. Provisions of new technologies and use of technology for obtaining information and communication for youth.
5. Development and promotion of book selection, interlibrary loan, collection development, and fee policies that include service to youth.

Youth Services Staff as Managers

1. Youth services librarians should have opportunities for involvement in local, area, and state boards, including boards and committees outside youth service.
2. Youth services librarians should be assertive as managers.
3. Youth services librarians should go outside parochial interest by showing interest in topics outside youth areas.
4. Youth services librarians should interact with committees and faculty in library schools and in teaching courses outside.

FOCUS 2

THE RIGHT STUFF: RECRUITMENT AND EDUCATION
FOR CHILDREN'S AND YOUNG
ADULT SPECIALISTS

Continuing Education

1. Create a clearinghouse of educational programs for youth specialists coordinated with CLENE.
2. Explore opportunities for teleconferencing and other alternative forms of continuing education.
3. Provide continuing education for all youth services workers.
4. Provide continuing education in related disciplines such as child psychology and management.
5. Develop ways of funding continuing education.

Youth Consultants

1. Provide a state level consultant in each state for youth services.
2. Work with the state board of education on coordinating programs between school and public libraries.
3. Link libraries with literacy efforts at state and regional levels to support the rationale for youth consultants.
4. Provide system and regional youth services consultants.
5. Develop a coalition of youth divisions in ALA and PLA.
6. Petition to adopt a youth agenda by ALA.

Standards

1. Develop a list of competencies for youth services workers.
2. Set standards for library and media center programs.
3. Explore the possibility of the construction of a national exam for youth service workers.
4. Gather data on the various state certification programs. Identify or develop a workable model for certification of school media specialists.
5. Examine and revise as necessary library school curricula related to youth services.

Image

1. Identify model individuals and programs in youth services and publicize them.
2. Be visible in nonyouth-oriented activities in the library profession.
3. Assume leadership roles in professional activities.

FOCUS 3
LIVING UP TO EXPECTATIONS: EVALUATION OF SERVICE TO CHILDREN AND YOUNG ADULTS

National Coordination

1. ALA divisions should gather, synthesize, and distribute local and/or state standards.
2. Adapt *Output Measures for Public Libraries* to youth services needs, recognizing that tools and standards can be used to justify effective budget results.
3. Include training for evaluation in library education and provide in-service training for youth service librarians on evaluation techniques.

Measurement

1. Develop measures of success in reaching target audiences.
2. Create a clearinghouse for samples of evaluations using qualitative and quantitative measurement techniques. Publish results of research related to youth services.
3. Hold a national program on this topic with representatives from other organizations concerned with evaluation.
4. Develop a research agenda for youth services.

Having developed a national youth agenda, it is time to develop a personal agenda, a commitment—to list the beginnings or continuations that you can make, for this is not a challenge to "they" but to "we." What will you do tomorrow? What will you do next week? Next month? Next year? As Gerald Hodges said: "We all need to establish priorities."

At the opening session Marilyn Miller said she hoped it wasn't a "freeze-dried" speech. I can say that I know this is not a freeze-dried agenda we are developing.

I'd like to share two final notable quotables, not from the Allerton Institute but two of my favorites. Both relate to attitude, often an overriding factor in the success of any venture. First, Henry Ford said: "If you think you *can* or if you think you *can't*, you're right!" Second, as Yoda said to Luke Skywalker: "There is not T-R-Y—there's only DO or NOT DO.

Let's do it!

CONTRIBUTORS

JOAN L. ATKINSON, Associate Professor, Graduate School of Library and Information Service, University of Alabama, Tuscaloosa, Alabama.

MARGARET BUSH, Assistant Professor, Graduate School of Library & Information Science, Simmons College, Boston, Massachusetts.

JULIE CUMMINS, Children's Services Consultant, Monroe County Library System, Rochester, New York.

JUDITH A. DRESCHER, Director of Libraries, Memphis/Shelby County Public Library and Information Center, Memphis, Tennessee.

LESLIE EDMONDS, Assistant Professor, Graduate School of Library and Information Science, University of Illinois at Urbana-Champaign.

RUTH FAKLIS, Youth Services Consultant, Suburban Library System, Burr Ridge, Illinois.

DAWN H. HELLER, Media Servies Coordinator, Riverside-Brookfield High School, Riverside, Illinois.

CRAIGHTON HIPPENHAMMER, Assistant Children's Services Manager, Cuyahoga County Public Library, Cleveland, Ohio.

GERALD G. HODGES, Assistant Professor, School of Library and Information Science, University of Iowa, Iowa City, Iowa.

MARGARET MARY KIMMEL, Professor, School of Library and Information Science, University of Pittsburgh, Pittsburgh, Pennsylvania.

FRANCES M. McDONALD, Associate Professor, Library Media Education, Mankato State University, Mankato, Minnesota.

MARILYN L. MILLER, Professor and Chair, Department of Information and Library Studies, University of North Carolina, Greensboro, North Carolina.

REGINA MINUDRI, Director, Berkeley [California] Public Library and President American Library Association.

DELORES ZACHARY PRETLOW, Supervisor of Media Services, Richmond Public Schools, Richmond, Virginia.

SUSAN ROSENZWEIG, Information Manager, Center for Early Adolescence, Chapel Hill, North Carolina.

HELEN LLOYD SNOKE, Professor, School of Library Science, University of Michigan, Ann Arbor, Michigan.

CHRISTY TYSON, Youth Services Consultant, Alabama Public Library Service (at the time of the Allerton Conference, Young Adult Services Coordinator at Spokane [Washington] Public Library).

JANA VARLEJS, Director, Professional Development Studies, School of Communication, Information and Library Studies, Rutgers, The State University of New Jersey.

INDEX